THE BEGGAR IV

Die Before Dying

B.T. Swami

HARI-NAMA PRESS

Hari-Nama Press gratefully acknowledges the BBT for the use of verses and purports from Srila Prabhupada's books. All such verses and purports are © Bhaktivedanta Book Trust International, Inc.

Internal photographs: ©2005 Darby Terry, All rights reserved. Courtesy of Ronin Photographic. ©2005 Subala, All rights reserved. Courtesy of Ecstatic Creations.

First printing 2005
Second edition: Amazon KDP 2020

Cover and interior design by Subala dasa / Ecstatic Creations

ISBN 9798643997030

THE BEGGAR IV

Die Before Dying

Dedication

I dedicate this book to my dear disciples Ekavira dasa and Vrajalila devi dasi, who acted as my caretakers during my illness.

"One who has cultured himself that these different activities of the material world have nothing to do with him, his only business is to become Krishna conscious. Then it is to be understood that he has conquered death even in this present life…This sort of equilibrium in the transcendental state of Krishna consciousness, *nirdosam*, faultless, it is called faultless life."

— Srila Prabhupada lecturing on
Bhagavad-gita 5.14-22

Contents

Acknowledgements 1

Foreword 3

Author's Preface 5

Introduction 7

Meditation 1:   I Died on August 5th 15

Meditation 2:   A Dead Man Walking 19

Meditation 3:   I Am Being Called by Two Different Agencies 25

Meditation 4:   Am I a Survivor? 31

Meditation 5:   Having Gratitude for the Present by Having
More Appreciation of the Past 37

Meditation 6:   We Bid Each Other Farewell
To Connect Deeper 43

Meditation 7:   The Comfortable Prisoner Does Not Have
a Passion for Elevation 47

Meditation 8:   Mother Watches with Great Concern
as We Misuse Our Free Will 55

Meditation 9:   Satisfied to Serve as a Stone in Vrndavana 59

Meditation 10: Die Before Dying 65

Meditation 11: Life Is Simply So Many Breaths 71

Meditation 12: Let Us Pray to Have Our Bodies Hijacked
by the Lord 77

Meditation 13: We Will All Very Soon Have a Special
Appointment with Death 81

Meditation 14: The Things We Leave Behind 87

Meditation 15: Why Be Afraid of Death? 91

Meditation 16: The Nine-fold Process of Full Surrender 99

Meditation 17: Being on Death Row 105

Meditation 18: We Must Die for Ourselves 111

Meditation 19: Death Can Be the Perfect Escape 117

Meditation 20: Cancer: An Offering of Tough Love 123

Meditation 21: Live Until Dying 131

Epilogue 137

Appendix A: Take the Name of the Lord and Die 141

Appendix B: Die to Live 145

Glossary 149

About the Author 153

Acknowledgements

I would sincerely like to thank Lila Katha dasi for the editing of the book; Subala dasa for layout and cover design; Daruka dasa for the wonderful photographs used throughout the book; and Kripa dasi and Aja dasa for final editing. I would especially like to thank my disciples in England and Australia for financing the printing of this book.

I would also like to express my deepest gratitude for the many doctors and nurses, allopathic as well as alternative practitioners in Mexico, Hawaii, Florida, and Washington D.C. who so magnanimously offered their services in trying to save my life. Most importantly, I want to thank the thousands of devotees around the world who consistently prayed for me during my entire health crisis. I have fallen in love or even deeper in love with all of you.

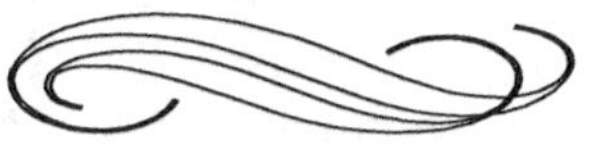

*T*he *Beggar IV: Die Before Dying* will take us on a spiritual journey into the heart of a man suddenly confronted by the mysteries of death. He does so with courage, compassion, and gratitude. Pouring from his heart is the message that successful life is not just in quantity of years, but in the substance of our wisdom, realizations, and love. Until we die to our selfish egotism, we cannot gain entrance into the abode of a true joyful life.

Bhakti Tirtha Swami has dedicated his life as a humble instrument of God's grace. His compassion for suffering humanity led him on a search for truth, which culminated in meeting his spiritual master, His Divine Grace A.C. Bhaktivedanta Swami Prabhupada. Over the years he has traveled the world extensively, taking incredible risks to share the gift of spiritual knowledge and love. He has penetrated the hearts of vast varieties of human beings, from tribal children in the jungles of Africa to the university professors of America. He inspires the hearts of forgotten destitutes dying in the ghettos as well as the most famous celebrities on earth. Presidents of nations, wealthy industrialists, abused children, and helpless widows have found hope and direction under the guidance of this selfless servant.

Bhakti Tirtha Swami has been a dearest friend to me for thirty-five years. I have witnessed his indomitable enthusiasm to inspire people's faith even in the face of indescribably complex circumstances. I have seen his heart weeping in compassion for the world's lost and suffering. His amazing creative genius has enthralled millions with timeless spiritual solutions to the problems of our contemporary world. Suddenly, at the age of 55 he was diagnosed with advanced melanoma cancer and given six months to live.

In this book, *The Beggar IV: Die Before Dying*, Bhakti Tirtha Swami lovingly shares his heart with us. He addresses the fears, struggles, and pains of facing imminent death. His honesty and faith will surely enlighten the minds and melt the hearts of the readers. With humility, gratitude, and joy he teaches us a way to welcome the loving hand of God. Let us carefully ponder the contents of this valuable treasure house of realizations.

I offer my deepest gratitude to Bhakti Tirtha Swami for this priceless contribution. I sincerely pray that all readers of this book may be inspired to rise above the superficialities of egoistic passions and sincerely follow the path of the saints, who die to live in the infinite bliss of God's love.

— His Holiness Radhanath Swami

Author's Preface

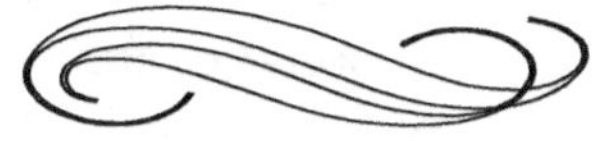

During the last six years, I intensified my traveling and started making world tours, often to nearly forty countries each year. Some days I would do as many as five or six programs per day. As I began to do more workshops and seminars centered on transformation, I began to look more closely at how intensely many people are suffering in secular communities as well as in spiritual communities. I became more determined to understand such sufferings and work to minimize them.

I prayed that whatever I needed to encounter to become fully pure in order to help others more profoundly come upon me. I wanted to assist devotees in having fewer encumbrances in their own spiritual pursuits for self-realization. Some short time later, almost out of nowhere, I was stricken with diabetes, prostate problems, anemia, insomnia, and advanced melanoma. I wrote these Beggar prayers as I struggled to survive the cancer—visiting Mexico, Hawaii, Palm Springs, and Washington D.C. for various treatments. I pray that these meditations will help those who are confronted with chronic illness or terminal sickness, as well as all other readers.

We are born to die, and death is around the corner for all of us. As I write this preface, I do not know if I will still be alive to see this book go to print. We have several other books which have already been written and are ready for print, but I let some of them wait in order to make this book available to the international community as soon as possible. Most of the prayers are listed in the order that they were written so as to help convey more of the spirit of my journey. The prayers in the Appendix are from *The Beggar I*; I included them again here because they are especially appropriate for this discussion. The reader should be able to connect very profoundly with the mind and heart of the author for the benefit of all.

These Beggar prayers have surely helped me to understand our inevitable appointment with death, and have helped me prepare to accept it with celebration. Hopefully they will educate and help prepare each of our readers as well for their appointment with death and that of their dear ones. If my *guru* and the Lord permit, hopefully I will still be alive and able to sign your book for you. But if not, please know that as you reflect on these prayers, from the spiritual realms I send you my love to comfort you through your own bewilderment, fear, anxiety, pain, and grief. Know that I love you dearly—yes, enough to die for you and others who are sincerely engaged in spiritual evolution.

I, the beggar, beg for your mercy and love, while I joyfully give you mine. You will feel my presence as you read these prayers—if you desire to.

The Beggar,
With love,
B.T. Swami

Introduction

Stop—yes, kindly hold on. Please! You are about to enter into sacred space: Death—the transition from here to there.

"Philosophy means to keep death in front of your eyes," said His Divine Grace A.C. Bhaktivedanta Swami, the author's spiritual master. Yes, death is not to be ignored. It can teach us important lessons for life, because death forces us to look for what is essential—something which still stands as important even before the scrutinizing eyes of the greatest of thinkers, who think everything to its final conclusion. Ultimately, death is always something very personal and private—like birth. Our own death will always be unique; different from everyone else's.

Bhakti Tirtha Swami has given us a unique gift, a gift which touches the heart: his own reflections about his own passing and how he prepares himself. It is a book relevant for all of us because we all will have to die. But, upon close reading you will soon discover that our author has "deceived" us. His book is really a book on living an empowered and empowering life, provided we take the implicit lessons to heart. "Die before dying" is a famous expression for the death of the false ego—a goal all spiritual traditions aim for.

Before our spiritual identity can emerge, our

false sense of who we are has to die. This false ego is compared with a knot in the heart, which binds the eternal soul to an illusory life. And this knot has to be cut. Once one has done this, one can easily see past the greatest illusion and recognize that actually there is no death. "For the soul there is neither birth nor death at any time. He has not come into being, does not come into being, and will not come into being. He is unborn, eternal, ever-existing and primeval. He is not slain when the body is slain" (*Bhagavad-gita* 2.20).

It is not that this subject is to be found exclusively in Vedic or Indian tradition. Christianity also speaks about the death of the old and sinful human, and the simultaneous birth of the new and better person (*Letter of the Romans* 6). The mystical traditions in Christianity know even of a *mors mystica*—the death of self-centered desires, which is necessary to enter our loving relationship with God. Once when the famous Master Eckhart was asked, "How should the person be, who can behold God?" he answered very simply, "He should be dead." He meant that the egomaniac has to die so that God can take control of our lives. Only then can we become His instruments.

The German poet Johann Wolfgang Goethe expressed it like this in *Blessed Longing*:

> And till you confront this test,
> This dying-and-becoming
> You'll only be a dismal guest
> At the earth's dim gloaming.

In the Vedic tradition, many *mantras* either to one's spiritual guide or to God Himself begin with the word *namah*—*na* meaning "not" and *mah* "me", which refers to the wrong conception of oneself as the body. *Namah* means "not me" and "not my desire", but "You Krishna and Your desire". Thus the syllable *namah* refers to the subject before us, the ego death.

Let me make it even clearer: the spiritual person will die two deaths. Just as it is important for the human being to take two births—one the physical and the other the spiritual—so he also has to go through two deaths. One is the death of the false ego and the other is the death of the coat—the material body. If one has overcome the false ego, the much feared physical death looses its horrors. When it occurs in the natural course of life, it can be as easy as moving from one room to the next, although it can also be accompanied by the dramatic drum beats of intense physical challenges—as God arranges. In any way, for a fully God conscious person there is nothing to fear, since with death he is moving only from one hand of God to the other.

Please do not be shocked or afraid when reading this: it is actually nice to die before dying. One can live a better and more fulfilled life after the ego has been unloaded. It is only by illusion that one thinks self-centered attachments are making one happy. Happiness always lies in freedom, not mental bondage. Isn't it a source of celebration when a prisoner can get rid of his prison life and start his real life? The best and most joyful example of "die before dying" is in my eyes the butterfly. Before going into the cocoon for his transformation, he is an earth-bound, ugly caterpillar, eating only dirt. After he has died before dying, he leaves the cocoon as a beautiful, colorful creature who roams in freedom through the air.

Unfortunately, many of us live in the prisons of our minds, and cannot imagine a life here and now in full bliss and knowledge. Enticed by a false sense of success and progress, we are not living according to our actual spiritual potential. This is brought to light by an unforgettable story that I would like to retell here:

Once there were two caterpillars, Trusty and Feary. They lived in a valley at the foothills of a mountain. One day the news came to them that at the end of their valley was a huge pillar which would lead to a life of total, instant fulfillment. One only had to climb it. Trusty and Feary were interested. They went there and found thousands of caterpillars trying to walk up the pillar. Finally they managed to get a place in line, and amongst the struggling, fighting, and pushing caterpillars, they began their way up. The pillar of progress had them.

Half way up, Trusty began to doubt their journey: "If everyone shoves and struggles and fights now to get to perfection, then I can't imagine that in the perfected place up there we will ever be friends. This is the wrong way of progress." When he told Feary, Feary saw his point, but was not willing to return. He argued: "If everyone climbs up the pillar of progress, then it must be good." Nevertheless, Trusty was determined to follow his inner conviction. So he said good-bye to Feary and climbed down the pillar.

After a long journey, Trusty reached his home in the valley. One day he heard a voice from a bush, "Hey, Trusty, look at me." When he looked up, he saw a caterpillar who was almost leaving his cocoon. "What are you doing?" The caterpillar looked at him and said, "I am going into the transformation; soon I will fly high into the sky."

Trusty said, "I just came from high up in the sky. It doesn't work." But the caterpillar had already closed the cocoon. One month later the cocoon opened up and when Trusty came, he could only see the white remains. Over night, when he was sleeping, his friend had turned into a butterfly and early in the morning flown to the flowers, where he drank deep from their flower juices.

Trusty was fascinated. He wanted to leave the earth, he wanted to be high in the sky, but it was clear to him that the pillar of progress could not provide that.

One day he decided to also climb on the bush, and when he saw that a thin silken thread came from his body, he went along with nature: He covered himself like he had seen his friend doing and one day left the cocoon as a beautiful butterfly. O, how happy he was to finally fulfill his desire—in a natural way.

Meanwhile on the pillar of progress, Feary was just before the end of the pillar. As he was making his way to the top, which was covered in a cloud, he heard voices above him—most disturbing voices: "Oh no, it's only a lie. We have been cheated." The next thing he heard was someone falling and crushing on the floor. "Oh no," said the voice, "again someone has fallen down and died. Soon I will be next." Then he heard another voice, "Don't speak so loud; the others could find out that we have only followed an illusion of progress and that we will soon all die."

Feary was in absolute terror. Just then he heard a voice, "Hey, Feary." When he looked to the side, he saw a beautiful creature with colorful wings, dancing around him in the air. "Hey Feary, it's me." Feary was fearful, "Who are you?" The strange and beautiful creature said, "Look into my eyes, Feary." When Feary looked deeply, he recognized his old friend and full of surprise he said, "Trusty, you have come at a very important stage of my life. Please help me; I am going to die. This pillar of success does not lead anywhere. Everyone is pushing upwards, but they all will fall down when they reach the goal. It's only fifty more centimeters before I, too, have to fall on the ground and die. Trusty said, "I have come to get you. Just trust me." Feary was happy. His friend would not betray him. Trusty then took him and brought him down to the ground. There he patiently taught him the art of transformation and soon also Feary entered the cocoon to die before dying. He dissolved his old ego of a caterpillar and emerged as a wonderful butterfly to fly in freedom.

This story tells us that, yes, in the beginning we might be shocked to hear about the book's title just as Feary was shocked. But if we take shelter under proper spiritual guidance and a genuine process, we will also learn to "freely fly in the spiritual sky" by transforming the ego and becoming a trusting, free soul.

Like no other author, Bhakti Tirtha Swami is specifically qualified to write about this sensitive subject. His words carry a specific weight due to his terminal cancer. To date, Bhakti Tirtha Maharaja has gone through five months of intense treatments, holistic and allopathic. After three blood transfusions, four operations, including an amputation, several emergency visits to various hospitals, weeks of residing in different hospitals with different types of treatments, it is sure: His survival rate is less than 10 percent. But Maharaja takes it in a spiritual way. His *mantra* is: "I am blessed by the best, would not settle for anything less, and I continue to pray to be able to pass the remaining tests."

This book is written with the ink of realization on the papers of real life. It is not a theoretical presentation for the entertainment of the illusion that we can live eternally in this world. At times it seems that the author walks out of the pages, grabbing his readers by the arm and pleading with them: "Now, use your time for your ultimate benefit. Don't be afraid of transformation."

As I am writing this I feel in my heart mixed emotions of gratitude, admiration, and love extending to our blessed Swami. Bhakti Tirtha Swami has always been an example and also challenge for me—a challenge for growth. I am one of the millions of people on this planet whose life has been permanently uplifted by him, and somehow I intuitively feel sure that whatever happens, we will meet again—either in this body or beyond, because ultimately no one dies. The soul is eternal, full of bliss and knowledge.

Bhakti Tirtha Maharaja has worked tirelessly in the service of his beloved spiritual master to bring this joyous message all around the world. This is yet another book with this joyful message: "Wake up, O eternal soul, to the land of spiritual freedom."

— His Holiness Sacinandana Swami

"All of us can decide to leave behind a life of mediocrity and to live a life of greatness. No matter what our circumstances may be, such a decision can be made by every one of us—whether that greatness is manifest by choosing to have a magnificent spirit in facing an incurable disease, by making a difference in the life of a child, by giving another person a sense of worth and potential, by becoming a change-catalyst inside an organization, or by becoming an initiator of a great cause in society."

— Stephen Covey

Meditation 1

I Died on August 5th

On August 5, 2004, I truly began the process of ending my existence on this planet in this body. During that week, I discovered that I had sugar diabetes and advanced melanoma. Prior to that time, I knew of other health problems, but they were insignificant in contrast to the new ones that had developed. The old health problems should have been enough in themselves to alert me that my body is very fragile. Just having a material body is itself a disease because the body incarcerates the soul and limits the soul from its most blissful, fulfilling activities.

Every day, people must confront the shocking

news that they or someone near to them has become possessed by a life threatening disease. When people have this encounter, they feel angry, bewildered, and cheated, wondering why it must happen to them. They would like to accept that these kinds of disasters happen to others and not to themselves. We forget that practically everyone who meets such a destiny is thinking the same: "Why has this happened to me instead of to someone else?" If each person had their wish, then these misfortunes would be experienced by others and never by themselves. The person who feels cheated is eager to project their own misfortune on others. Such people are concerned about not being cheated themselves while being eager to cheat others.

People normally feel some happiness, even if others are suffering, as long as they are not personally experiencing any difficulties. How wonderful it would be if we could think of ourselves as fortunate when we are chosen to experience challenges for our growth, which can relieve another from having to undergo the same difficulties. This, of course, is the mood of a high-class devotee who is *para-duhkha-duhkhi*. A devotee feels the miseries of others and enjoys their happiness with them.

The feelings of anger and bewilderment are due to not understanding that the Supreme Lord's mercy comes in many different ways. It is easy to accept God's mercy when we get what we want. This is like mercy coming from the front. However, when it comes from the side, it can be bewildering, and even more so when it comes from behind. When it comes from behind, it can be extremely disturbing because the conditioned *jiva* loves to feel that he or she is in control. This, of course, is a big illusion, for we are always at the mercy of the Lord. However, we normally think that we are much more in control than we really are. Actually, the Lord's mercy coming from behind, as in the case of an apparent calamity, is even more an expression of the Lord's mercy because, in such instances, the Lord helps the *jiva* to accept and perceive her eternal identity as a wonderfully dependent servant.

We must remind ourselves that the Lord is always finding ways to send out His love. As we remind ourselves of this, it becomes easier to take advantage of the many opportunities that manifest. Life is full of adventures and opportunities to serve humanity and glorify the Lord. When a person can accept everything as an expression of Krishna's mercy and love, nothing can be too disturbing. Every moment becomes another opportunity to serve humanity, worship the Supreme, and express gratitude.

August 5th was truly a rebirth, for it gave me a chance to die to live. I, the beggar, am full of gratitude for receiving the Lord's mercy from the front, from all sides, and yes, most wonderfully, from the back.

Meditation 2

A Dead Man Walking

Have you seen the dead man walking? He is very eager to identify with relatives, describing himself as a member of a particular continent, country, race, gender, and age group. He has pictures of all his family members and they have pictures of him. They have family reunions where members of the family from all over the country show up to discuss the latest family gossip. They talk about who died and who was born that year, who got married and who divorced. Each year he wonders who will be the next person to leave their body. *Perhaps it will be him, for he is a dead man who is still walking.*

He goes to work early in the morning and returns very late in the evening. His wife and children seem happier when he leaves the house than when he returns. He hates his job and feels that his boss and colleagues probably dislike him as much as he dislikes them. Still, he must continue going to work every day, but each year he wonders who will be the next colleague to leave their body. *Perhaps it will be him, for he is a dead man who is still walking.*

He puts away money for car insurance, house insurance, and life insurance. Several of his associates have been in car accidents, natural disasters have destroyed their houses, and some lost their family members due to accidents and disease. He has very good insurance and feels that he will be ready whenever such calamities assault his possessions, relatives, or himself. However, he doesn't like surprises and wonders when some or all of those calamities will visit him. *He is trying to realize that there is no reason to be disturbed or caught off-guard, for he is already a dead man walking.*

Sometimes he thinks about changing professions or going back to school to take another degree. He was reflecting on how the average person in the United States changes cars every three to four years, houses every seven, professions about four times in a lifetime, and jobs about ten times in a lifetime. It seemed obvious to him that everything and everybody is constantly changing. *Each year he wonders what will next change in his life, for he is a dead man who is still walking.*

Every Sunday he goes to church, synagogue, mosque, or temple to see mostly the same people doing the same things. Sometimes he wonders how much they actually believe and truly understand what they are doing. The songs and prayers are sung and chanted; the scripture is read; and the sermon is given. Every other month or so, there is a funeral as a member of the congregation passes on. Sometimes he is apprehensive to go to the place of worship, knowing that he will hear more names of those who have recently passed. *However, he also knows that the church, synagogue, mosque, or temple will some day announce his departure, for he is a dead man who is still walking.*

He had been very lonely in the past, but then he met his wife. He expected her to make him happy and totally satisfied. He was sure that she would make this important miracle happen in his life. The problem, however, is that she was expecting the same thing from him. They each wanted happiness and satisfaction from the other. What they ultimately got was disappointment and frustration because neither was ready to accommodate the needs of the other. Each expected the other to facilitate personal needs.

The dead man walking is actually every one of us because we are all likely to overly identify with bodily distinctions involving race, nationality, gender, politics, family, job, security, education, rituals, and romance. We often view these distinctions as the essence of life, considering everything else to be secondary. While so absorbed, we tend to forget that all of these concerns are relative and temporary. In time, we will change, others will change, and circumstances will be different. Most important, death will arrive soon even if someone lives in this body for a long time—even 100 years is still a short period. Death is inevitable, and is just around the corner for each and every person.

So whether a man lives for one year or 100, he is a dead man walking, for death is coming very soon. Death shall not only change all things, but shall be the final reward and the final experience. We might think that our present existence, identities, and relationships will continue indefinitely as they are, but soon they will all be in the past. We are just moments from death.

If you did not notice the dead man walking, it is because you have not observed others closely. Even worse, you have not been honest in observing yourself. *Keep on walking, achieving, excelling, relating, and reflecting, for soon you will fully recognize that you are that dead man walking.*

I am the beggar who has realized that he is a dead man walking.

Meditation 3

I Am Being Called by Two Different Agencies

How wonderful it is to have so many friends and associates who care for me so dearly and who are so eager for me to be with them, even though I am most unworthy of their association. They are most kind and tolerant, constantly extending their mercy to me in many different ways. This imposes a problem because my associates who know me in this lifetime have their reasons for wanting me to continue existing here, but my friends and associates who know me eternally also have their reasons for wanting me to close this chapter of my existence and join them in other services. Both groups are convincing, but who am I to decide which decision should be honored, and who am I to decide which will be more pleasing to my spiritual master? *Therefore, I submit myself to my Gurudeva, asking him to guide me according to what he feels is necessary and best in his service to humanity.*

My relatives, friends, and associates here are concerned that I am needed in my relationships with them because we share something unique and important together. But my relatives, friends, and associates in the higher realms are even more convinced that it is now necessary for me to join them because we share something even more unique and important together. *Therefore, I submit myself to my Gurudeva, asking him to guide me according to what he feels is necessary and best in his service to humanity.*

My relatives, friends, and associates here feel that since I have so many family members and disciples who are connected to me and who depend on me, it would be unhealthy to separate myself from them. Their contention is that, as I am the baby in this family, it is unnatural for the youngest amongst the children to be the first to leave the body. As far as my disciples all around the world, they feel that they are still too much like babies and very much still need the physical presence of their spiritual master. *Therefore, I submit myself to my Gurudeva, asking him to guide me according to what he feels is necessary and best in his service to humanity.*

My relatives, friends, and associates here say that I have so many of my spiritual master's books to distribute and so many of my own books to finish writing and publishing. My spiritual master honored me as one of his biggest book distributors, and I also have my own different series of books with additional volumes to complete. They feel I cannot depart so soon for I will leave these series incomplete, and I also still have thousands of people to introduce to my spiritual master's books. *Therefore, I submit myself to my Gurudeva, asking him to guide me according to what he feels is necessary and best in his service to humanity.*

My relatives, friends, and associates here say that I must surely continue offering my seminars, workshops, and media appearances since they are beneficial and help many devotees and non-devotees transform themselves into better people with much greater sensitivity and compassion. *Therefore, I submit myself to my Gurudeva, asking him to guide me according to what he feels is necessary and best in his service to humanity.*

My relatives, friends, and associates here say that we have so many temples to maintain, farm communities to develop, and other preaching projects to expand. There are so many demons and *mayavadis* to expose and bewildered people to save. Most people in society today are controlled by propaganda, fads, lust, and greed. Most people live only for improving their mating and defending. Some who are a little more evolved pursue various religious activities for improving their material condition. However, involvement in *dharma* (religiosity), *artha* (economic development), *kama* (sense gratification), and *moksa* (liberation) are all inferior to *sanatana-dharma* or transcendental activities. *Therefore, I submit myself to my Gurudeva, asking him to guide me according to what he feels is necessary and best in his service to humanity.*

My relatives, friends, and associates from the higher realms are requesting that I come back to join them, as I have many duties awaiting me such as festivals to help arrange, special *prasadam* to prepare, cows to take care of, dances to participate in, and associates who are eager for me to bathe in the bliss of unconditional service with them. Although they are happy to see me engaged in the lower realms, exposing the demons, preaching to the bewildered, and encouraging the pious, they have reminded me that these activities are still associated with the material worlds. These activities give great mercy to the conditioned souls, but such activities can cause one to feel like the controller or feel that the goal of spiritual life is combating negativity. In fact, the essence of spirituality is not to fight the deviants, convert others, or engage in varieties of preaching endeavors, although these are very important. These activities are an integral part of the mission of the *gosthy-anandis*. Lord Caitanya has requested that this message be delivered to every town and village, which is the mood of most of our great *acaryas*. However, more important than these activities is returning back to our original home in the spiritual world where every moment is a joyful and animated opportunity to serve and glorify the Divine Couple.

My relatives, friends, and associates from the higher realms reminded me that if I am to remain longer in the material universes on various preaching missions, I must remain constantly aware of the actual goal of all spiritual activities and I must be extremely careful to not minimize the importance of being fully absorbed and surrendered in the mood of a *vrajavasi*. I must be careful to not preach about Vrndavana while living more as an agent of *dharma* or religiosity. How fortunate I feel that I am being considered and invited by my relatives, friends, and associates from the material worlds as well as the higher realms. I am prepared to stay or leave. *Therefore, I submit myself to my Gurudeva, asking him to guide me according to what he feels is necessary and best in his service to humanity.*

I am that beggar who is desperate—who is being called to stay and also to return home. My dear spiritual master, you can keep me here or send me home according to whichever gives you and humanity the greatest service.

Meditation 4

Am I a Survivor?

Violence and war are prevalent all over the planet. Every few seconds, one person is murdering another somewhere in this world. With the introduction of television in many countries, the murder rate has doubled within the last fifteen years. One living entity is food for another. Not only do different nations attack each other, but members of the same ethnic groups, institutions, religious groups, and even families are constantly in conflict. The greatest violence is often the violence each individual perpetrates on him or herself through addictions, bad habits, and unhealthy lifestyles. The violence turned inwards on oneself produces depression and physical sickness.

One of the greatest sicknesses is cancer, which is among the world's greatest threats to a healthy physical existence. It is no accident that many people develop cancer after a great trauma in their lives such as the death of a dear one, a divorce, or the loss of an important job. In these cases, a very upsetting event causes the mind to experience great disturbances, and such mental energy sends unhealthy messages that cause the various organs and tissues in the body to attack each other.

Cancer cells are like intruding enemies that are trained for espionage. They sneak into the body, often hiding for many years to later surface with great destructive power, just as *maya* or evil is always around and waiting for an opportunity to capitalize whenever there is a weakness. So I am amongst the hundreds of millions of people attacked by cancer. Presently, tens of millions who are attacked by cancer have died, tens of millions are dying, and millions are seeing themselves as cancer survivors. It is, however, an illusion that someone thinks they have survived cancer, or any attack of death, for no one actually defeats or conquers death. *At best, we only postpone the inevitable, for death is still around the corner.*

Sometimes we hear people explain that they are survivors of alcoholism, child abuse, abandonment by their parents, rape, battery, and other painful experiences. But actually, none of these people are survivors, for each has been traumatized by their difficulty even though they have somewhat passed through these devastating experiences. Each person is marked by their past, and each person still carries impressions and wounds from their challenges into the present.

Many people meet regularly in support groups to check-in and discuss how they are five year, ten year, or fifteen year survivors. It is wonderful that such support groups help people to be open and honest about their most difficult challenges. It is also very wonderful that such people can have a safe environment where they can discuss their problems with people who not only understand but fully empathize with them. However, many of these people have no identity other than being a survivor of a particular trauma. Constantly accepting and identifying themselves with the trauma can make them stagnant, and they may find that their whole lives revolve around that which has traumatized them. Their identity as a survivor is ambiguous because no one has really survived anything; their experiences remain a part of their consciousness and impact their being. Even if the experiences did not bring immediate devastation, death is still in the near future for all of us. No one actually defeats or conquers death. *At best, we only postpone the inevitable, for death is still around the corner.*

Many times people think that they will very easily survive a challenge—even an operation. The teacher, supervisor, or doctor may say that it is a very easy or ordinary experience to pass through, but often the person still fails or the patient dies. Other times, the teacher, supervisor, or doctor explains how it is a most difficult situation with a slim chance of survival; however, the person not only avoids death, but he or she comes out of the situation with great success. The ultimate outcome always depends on the Lord.

Very few people these days are surviving the devastating effects of orthodox society. The attacks which come from gambling, meat-eating, intoxication, and illicit sex have fully captured most living entities. These great enemies basically enslave people because most accept these influences gladly. Actually, it is difficult for someone to avoid their influences and enslavements. *Maya* or illusion is stronger than anyone because she is a perfect servant of the Lord whose duty is to test the *jivas* and to prepare them to eventually return back to the spiritual world. Therefore, no one can defeat her alone. She is surely an equal opportunity employer who does not discriminate.

> *daivi hy esa guna-mayi*
> *mama maya duratyaya*
> *mam eva ye prapadyante*
> *mayam etam taranti te*

This divine energy of Mine, consisting of the three modes of material nature, is difficult to overcome. But those who have surrendered unto Me can easily cross beyond it.

Bhagavad-gita 7.14

When *maya* attacks, it is difficult for anyone to defeat or conquer her influences. However, with sufficient help from Krishna and His special servants, *maya* can easily be avoided and will even become a servant of such a devotee. When the fortunate living entity is blessed with special mercy, the great gift of *prema* descends upon him or her. Such a devotee will also not survive because this special mercy will change him forever. Having come in contact with *bhava* and *prema* just once, the devotee's life will never be the same again.

If you are indeed attached to your worldly friends, do not look at the smiling face of Lord Govinda as He stands on the bank of the Yamuna at Kesighata. Casting sidelong glances, He places His flute to His lips, which seem like newly blossomed twigs. His transcendental body, bending in three places, appears very bright in the moon-light.

Caitanya-caritamrta Adi-lila 5.224

Also, if one is fortunate to get a moment's association with a pure devotee of the Lord, this will be their greatest benediction:

'sadhu-sanga',
'sadhu-sanga'—sarva-sastre kaya
lava-matra sadhu-sange sarva-siddhi haya

The verdict of all revealed scriptures is that by even a moment's association with a pure devotee, one can attain all success.

Caitanya-caritamrta Madhya-lila 22.54

This is the real purport of being a "survivor." A genuine survivor is one who can say, "I am a survivor of Krishna's and the pure devotee's special mercy. Just as violence can descend on one through all types of inauspicious attacks, just as cancer is attacking millions of people, just as all kinds of traumatic experiences can affect people throughout their lives, just as people come together in survivor and support groups, we must develop the consciousness of pleading for our material consciousness to be attacked and traumatized by the experience of *bhava* and *krsna-prema*.

How wonderful to be counted amongst those who will be able to say, "I am a survivor of Krishna's and the pure devotee's special mercy." All other areas from which we think we survive and free ourselves from the difficulties are only temporary because death will still find a way to defeat us. For the most fortunate *jiva* who is traumatized by the mercy of the Supreme Lord, he is permanently affected in the most glorious way. Such a soul can be a part of the transcendental support groups that are commissioned by the Lord and His eternal associates. They have many realizations, experiences, and pastimes to share with each other and with all who are fortunate enough to get their association.

I, the beggar, pray that one day I can say that I am a recipient—a survivor—of the blessings of *prema* from the Lord and His pure devotees who are the authorized carriers and distributors of such mercy. I, the beggar, am praying to be divinely traumatized by the mercy and love of the Lord and His pure devotees.

Meditation 5

Having Gratitude for the Present by Having More Appreciation of the Past

It is easy to take so much for granted—even life itself. Normally when we have opportunities, facilities, or experiences, we can easily fail to appreciate them fully; however, when we no longer have them, we are often forced to reflect more on how we benefited from what we had in the past.

I may presently find myself in a situation of loss. In this situation, I can become very angry, sad, and depressed, or I can become more attentive, appreciative, and full of gratitude. *When people reflect on past commodities, experiences, facilities, opportunities, and associations, they can relive and recapture their beauty, feeling grateful for what was available in the past.*

I have come down with a chronic disease, which is obviously very devastating. However, the extreme inconvenience and pain created by the present situation can spark much more appreciation for the many years I had in the past without illness. *How happy, appreciative, and full of gratitude I can feel as I recapture and relive the beauty of the past, bringing that beauty, happiness, and satisfaction into the present.*

We might have difficulty eating or sleeping, but we can reflect on how fortunate and wonderful the experiences were when we were able to eat sumptuous foodstuff of different varieties and how pleasant it was to have nights of deep, restful and peaceful sleep. By such reflections of gratitude, we can bring forth those past experiences into the present. *We can be grateful for the past and most grateful for the present.*

Presently we may not be able to participate in mating or defending; however, we can be grateful to not be encumbered in this way. We can appreciate our present simplified situation as well as bring forth past happiness, success, and achievements with full gratitude as a way to recapture and relive the healthy experiences in our present moments. *In this way, we can be grateful for the past and most grateful for the present.*

Presently I may have difficulty talking or walking. I can become very angry, sad, or depressed, or I can experience great appreciation and gratitude for the past achievements, bringing them fully into the present. We can go into a deep reflection on the pleasant accomplishments of the past, reliving and recapturing these experiences with full gratitude and appreciation. *By such reflections of gratitude, we can bring forth these past experiences into the present, feeling grateful for the past and most grateful for the present.*

Perhaps I may have difficulty seeing, hearing, tasting, and feeling. These difficulties can make me very angry, sad, and depressed, or I can experience great appreciation and gratitude for past reflections which involved healthy sensual experiences— seeing wonderful sights, hearing beautiful sounds, tasting wonderful goodies, and feeling delightful sensations. By such reflections of gratitude, we can bring the dynamic impacting experiences from the past into the present. *In this way, we can be grateful for the past and most grateful for the present.*

Perhaps now I am not able to travel around the world as I used to. I can become very angry, sad, and depressed, or I can experience great appreciation for the opportunities to visit so many countries and associate with so many wonderful devotees in each country. How much happiness, appreciation, and gratitude I can have by bringing so many wonderful, dynamic, and exciting experiences from the past into the present and future. *In this way, we can be grateful for the past and most grateful for the present.*

It is surely very easy to take natural and wonderful situations, experiences, accomplishments, facilities, and associations for granted, especially when the present is problematic. We can absorb ourselves with the present limitations, restrictions, setbacks, and disappointments, or we can remind ourselves that the Supreme Lord is always our well-wisher who is constantly arranging everything for our benefit. It is easy to accept this when everything is going on according to our desires, but most difficult when we have to deal with seemingly unpleasant experiences.

We have had so many wonderful opportunities to engage in service in the past; we have so many present experiences, opportunities, and challenges; and we will have many amazing adventures, experiences, and challenges in the future. Each encounter, association, and experience is ultimately wonderful and arranged by Krishna for our benefit. It is naturally difficult to maintain this constant awareness when we allow ourselves to dwell on our challenges, but by developing gratitude for the past and gratitude for the present, we can live every day and every moment as pleasant, exciting, rewarding, fulfilling and meaningful experiences.

Life is full of meaning and opportunities for growth. When we are mindful of the beauty and accomplishments of the past, even when the present or future is not exactly what we would like it to be, we will not be disturbed. We will still be excited about the past and appreciative for the present. In this way, the future will be even more auspicious because we create our futures by how we have dealt with the past and how we are dealing with the present. Being always reflective, mindful, and grateful allows us to never forget how much the Supreme Lord is sending His love in different ways.

I am that beggar who is looking very closely at the past with utmost appreciation, which is giving me greater gratitude about the present and extreme excitement about the future.

Meditation 6

We Bid Each Other Farewell–
To Connect Deeper

When we greet someone, we are honoring their presence and recognizing their existence in connection with ours. We are accepting them into our reality. When we bid someone farewell, we are normally doing the opposite; we are separating ourselves as they are separating themselves from us. A farewell establishes a formal recognition to alter the relationship, to dismiss oneself from the environment, and to honor another's dismissal.

When I was told that I had advanced melanoma and might have only six months to live, I began to think of all the people in my life to whom I should bid farewell, but did I actually want to dismiss myself from them or them from me? It seemed that instead I wanted to be more present in their lives and I wanted them to be more present in mine.

My biological family members telephoned me several times, one by one expressing their kind thoughts and prayers. Later my immediate brother and sisters came to visit me for a few days. We laughed and cried together, and reflected on many things dear to all of us, especially my departed mother, who was highly spiritual and who so lovingly inspired all of us.

As we talked and prayed together, we could feel my mother's presence with us. My brother and sisters all bonded so nicely and then focused their collective attention and affection on me. They all knew that this could possibly be the last time we would be together, so we were very happy for each moment we had. It was as if we were all experiencing each other's sweetness and love for the first time. I thought, how wonderful for Krishna to have given me such a variegated, charming, and spiritual biological family. I am the baby in the family of two brothers and four sisters. This, of course, surrounded me with the loving affection a spoiled younger sibling would hope for. *Although we bid each other farewell, we really wanted to connect on a deeper level, not actually desiring to dismiss ourselves from each other. I wondered why it could not always be like this.*

Many of my old friends that I grew up with called me. Some I had not heard from for many years. They had heard that I might be leaving my body soon and wanted to reflect on our past association. We shared how much we benefited from each other and how much we would miss each other. It was as if we were discovering each other's sweetness and love for the first time. We laughed and cried together. *Although we bid each other farewell, we really wanted to connect on a deeper level, not actually desiring to dismiss ourselves from each other. I wondered why it could not always be like this.*

I was so fortunate to get visits and phone calls from godbrothers and godsisters from all over the world. It was wonderful. We shared pastimes of our *guru* and of the preaching we had done together. We recounted conflicts and problems we faced together, and shared realizations and deep appreciations of each other. We laughed and cried together in exchanges that were remarkably powerful, sweet, and loving. It was as if we were discovering each other's sweetness and love for the first time. Reflecting on Krishna's and Srila Prabhupada's mercy for bringing us all together as spiritual generals to work for them was overwhelming. *Visit after visit, phone call after phone call, we bid each other farewell, not actually desiring to dismiss each other, but really wanting to connect on a deeper level. I wondered why it could not always be like this.*

I was so fortunate to get visits, telephone calls, and letters from my disciples all around the world. It was wonderful as we shared deep, loving sentiments. We discussed our pastimes and associations together. We laughed and cried together. My words and writings penetrated deep into their hearts, and their loving prayers reached deep into the chambers of my heart, never to leave. It was as if we were discovering each other's sweetness and love for the first time, not knowing if death would come to me soon. *Although we bid each other farewell, we really wanted to connect on a deeper level,*

*not actually desiring to dismiss ourselves from
each other. I wondered why it could not always be
like this.*

We have many associations that have always
been wonderful, but we often appreciate them
more when there is some tragedy, abrupt change,
or intense challenge in our life or someone else's.
Many of these changes make us feel as if we are
encountering each other in a wonderfully revealing
and joyful presence for the first time. It is at times
when we have to bid each other farewell that we
connect on a deeper level than we had during our
previous associations. The science of *vipralambha*,
intense love in separation, is awesome. When we
are mindful and appreciative while we are with our
beloved, each moment can be as powerful as the
profound connection that is experienced when we
are anticipating separation.

As I wonder why it cannot always be like this, I,
the beggar, am now aware that in fact it can always
be like this. You and I can make it like this by
always bidding each other farewell in our minds,
not desiring to dismiss each other, but actually
capturing each moment as if it could be the last.

Meditation 7

The Comfortable Prisoner Does Not Have a Passion for Elevation

The *svarupa-laksana*, the essential aspect of devotional service, is to have full dependence on Krishna and to never forget Him. Rupa Gosvami, the great renunciate from Vrndavana, explains the importance of fully depending on Krishna as the foremost tenet of advancing in Krishna consciousness. When we do not sufficiently depend on Krishna, we think of ourselves as the controllers and we interfere with Krishna's mercy, blessings, empowerment, and love descending upon us.

The material world and the material body are designed to create an arena where the living entities can try to think of themselves as separate from

Krishna without recognizing His supreme control over all things. Such thinking means that they will continue to undergo repeated birth and death, captivated by illusions of material culture. Conversely, as the living entities give up the artificial tendency to be the supreme controllers, they will become properly situated in transcendence. A great danger lies in remaining too comfortable and in experiencing only ordinary encounters in our lives. *When we live an ordinary life, we are more likely to accept the illusions of the material body, and we are more likely to be satisfied as prisoners in the material world who are away from our true home—the kingdom of God. The comfortable prisoner does not have the pressure to achieve liberation.*

In the material world, people are very desperate to become rich with much opulence (*aisvarya*). They want to acquire as many assets as possible because having such things makes them feel powerful. With their money, they can influence all kinds of people and situations. The power associated with wealth can be very intoxicating and can cause a person to feel an unhealthy dominance over others. *Consequently, they can fall into a dangerous position of finding satisfaction as a prisoner in the material world, away from their true home—the kingdom of God. After all, the comfortable prisoner does not have the passion for liberation.*

In the material world, people desperately try to make themselves beautiful (*sri*). They go out of their way to buy lovely and expensive clothes; they pay for fancy hairdos; and pay exorbitantly for plastic surgery. Those who are considered most beautiful participate in beauty pageants or act as models, which can be very intoxicating for those involved. Others will admire, lust after, and seek them out, relating to them based on their attractive and captivating bodily features. It reinforces the illusion that there is some great perfection in having an attractive temporary body. It is surely temporary because no matter how attractive people may be, in time their bodies will deteriorate and the same people who were so captivated by their own image will find their bodies becoming repulsive. *Having highly attractive features and investing excessive time in increasing that attractiveness can be very dangerous for it can cause people to find satisfaction in remaining a prisoner in the material world, away from our true home—the kingdom of God. After all, the comfortable prisoner does not have the passion for liberation.*

In the material world, people are eager to become famous (*yasah*). They are starving for attention and will often go to any means to become the center of attention. We normally do not realize how much we deny, sabotage, exploit, and manipulate others for our own selfish reasons. One can justify all kinds of deviation when the ego is totally intoxicated by distinction and adoration. When one has achieved great fame, it can be even worse because such a person is likely to be condescending towards others, and will have trouble honoring criticism as well. *Fame can be very dangerous for it can cause people to find more satisfaction in remaining a prisoner in the material world, away from our true home—the kingdom of God. After all, the comfortable prisoner does not have the passion for liberation.*

In the material world, people want to be very strong (*virya*), and they want to be in association of others who have great power and strength so they can steal power from them. Those who are strong are feared, and they have their way. Since others do not challenge them as much, they bully others more. Their strength often causes them to not sufficiently appreciate another person's contribution. Their own strength makes them minimize being a team player. When people have a reputation for strength although they are actually weak, they try to cover up their weaknesses and consequently do not open themselves up to receive help. They think that no one else is in a proper position to help them. *Strength can be very dangerous for it can cause people to find more satisfaction in remaining a prisoner in the material world, away from our true home—the kingdom of God. After all, the comfortable prisoner does not have the passion for liberation.*

In the material world, people are often eager to show how much knowledge (*jnana*) they have. One person tries to show their knowledge by defeating another through debate or by collecting excessive amounts of information. There is much information available, but there is a shortage of knowledge and wisdom. Information without knowledge makes one proud. *This can be very dangerous for it can cause people to find more satisfaction in remaining a prisoner in the material world, away from our true home—the kingdom of God. After all, the comfortable prisoner does not have a passion for liberation.*

In the material world, people are eager to demonstrate their renunciation (*vairagya*). Such people proudly want to show how they have so much self-control and that they are detached. Mainly they are eager for it to be known that, while others are so disturbed, they are special in as much as they are much more wealthy, beautiful, famous, and strong than others. They feel themselves to be naturally superior and, therefore, detached and renounced. This so-called great renunciation is an expression of great false ego and again a tendency to see oneself as a controller. *Therefore, it can be very dangerous for it can cause people to find more satisfaction in remaining a prisoner in the material world, away from our true home—the kingdom of God. After all, the comfortable prisoner does not have a passion for liberation.*

The opulences of wealth (*aisvarya*), beauty (*sri*), fame (*yasah*), strength (*virya*) knowledge (*jnana*), and renunciation (*vairagya*) are actually the qualities that Krishna possesses in full: *krsnas tu bhagavan svayam*. Krishna is equipped fully with all of the opulences. It is natural that these opulences are sought after as they are most attractive, but since the Supreme is the most attractive, no one has opulences greater than Him. The nature of the conditioned soul is that he wants to act as the lord. He is full of the energy of God and therefore wants to be the most attractive. When the living entity is in possession of any of these opulences or focuses on trying to acquire them, even if he becomes a high achiever in any or all of these areas, it can be most dangerous because the *jiva* can increase his false ego and most unfortunately increase his illusion of being the controller.

The *svarupa-laksana* is full dependence on Krishna. To depend fully on Krishna and always think of Him is the essence of *bhakti-yoga* and of the science of giving up false proprietorship. All things that reinforce our false identification with the material body and the material world incarcerate us more in the material prison. By thinking of ourselves as controllers, we keep interfering with

Krishna's mercy, blessings, empowerment, and love descending upon us. When we are confronted with chronic illness and other great challenges; when we are not just pursuing an ordinary life; and when we are not overly intoxicated in trying to possess the opulences of Krishna, we are great candidates for becoming first class *bhaktas*. It is the mercy of *guru* and Krishna, who remind us from time to time that we are not the controllers. Thus, we can depend more on their guidance, empowerment, and mercy while appreciating Krishna's all-attractive opulences.

I, the beggar, am full of gratitude that *guru* and Krishna have forced me to better see that I am not the controller, so as to be a less comfortable prisoner in the material world. Therefore, my chances of returning back to the spiritual world have increased profoundly.

Meditation 8

Mother Watches with Great Concern as We Misuse Our Free Will

Mothers are very special, for they are nurturers, comforters, and facilitators. They have special relationships with their sons just as fathers have special relationships with their daughters. The Vedas explain that mothers normally make a greater impact on the personality of the son, and the father a greater impact on the daughter.

There are a lot of mothers in pain due to their own son or someone else's son who has put them in anxiety. The wife who is battered by her husband is suffering at the hands of someone's son. Her own son who gets angry so fast and resorts to violence repeatedly puts her and others in great anxiety.

In spite of these tremendous difficulties, the mother prays for everyone's well-being.

There is a mother out there whose son has been sent to prison. When she goes to visit him and talks to him through the barrier, she cries due to the pain she feels as she studies his predicament. *She wonders how he could abuse his free will to such an extent.*

There is a mother out there whose son received great affection and attention throughout his life. As he got older, she was excited to watch him mature. However, after he entered adolescence, his entire personality changed. He started coming home intoxicated, hiding what he was doing and what was happening to him. Later, he did not even seem to care if she noticed his intoxicated state. *She wonders how her son could abuse his free will to such an extent.*

There is a mother out there whose son has estranged himself from his family. He is constantly rushing off to join his friends and go to all kinds of events. Even when he agrees to come home for a meal, he rarely follows through. It is as if he purposely avoids associating with his family members. Whenever the family sits at the table to eat, his seat remains vacant. Even when he joins on those rare occasions, he leaves after only a few minutes or comes at the end of the meal. The family members, especially his mother, so much want him to include himself in family affairs. *She wonders how her son could abuse his free will to such an extent.*

There is a mother out there whose son has a chronic physical disease. She has taken him to doctors and healers, and although they all say that they can surely heal him, his sickness returns in one form or another. She sees so many other parents who have healthy children, but her poor son must suffer so tremendously. Her son often wonders why God has made him and his mother so unfortunate. He, of course, is suffering, and because he is so angry, he tries to make life miserable for everyone else as much as he can. He often goes out of his way to inflict pain on others. *His mother is sympathetic to his sickness, but wonders how her son could abuse his free will to such an extent.*

There is a mother out there whose son is extremely depressed. Not only is he always sad, but he seems the most miserable when everyone else seems happy and excited. He often complains to her about bringing him into this miserable world, frequently speaks about committing suicide, and has tried to take his life twice. *His mother, who loves him so much, wonders how her son could abuse his free will to such an extent.*

There is a Divine Mother out there who is most nurturing and compassionate. She watches Her sons experience moods of anger and confusion. She tries to remind Her sons and daughters why and how they have been sent to this material prison. Most importantly, She explains how to get out of this prison of birth, death, and desire once and for all, but nonetheless continues to watch Her children become more and more intoxicated by various illusions. This Mother is concerned about our unhealthy lifestyles. She is vigilant, anxious for the return of Her children. It intensely disturbs Her to see Her children physically and mentally sick.

That great nurturing and comforting Mother is none other than the Divine Mother, Srimati Radharani. She is the *hladini-sakti*, the divine eternal pleasure potency of the Lord, and the eternal

Mother God of all creations who is simultaneously the same and different from Father God, Sri Krishna. She is amazed at how we have turned our backs on our wonderful home in the spiritual world that She offers and maintains for us. Especially as we go through our chronic sicknesses and suicidal endeavors, it pains Her to see us in the difficult positions we have created for ourselves. She prays for our well-being, and makes arrangements for our return to our family where we no longer abuse our free will. Abuse of our free will is our most serious problem. All things have been lovingly arranged for us, but we have avoided, taken for granted, and exploited the profound mercy made available.

Dear Divine Mother God, I am the beggar, one of your sons, who is an offender in all of these areas. Please forgive me for denying, avoiding, abusing, and exploiting Your mercy. I am a poor example of a son, but the extent of Your loving, nurturing, and comforting is beyond my comprehension. Please do not give up on me, even though it is me who keeps abusing my free will.

Meditation 9

Satisfied to Serve as a Stone in Vrndavana

Sometimes we think of service to Krishna as only being possible in the human form of life. This can cause us to minimize how Krishna extends Himself in many variegated ways to all species. He not only provides opportunities for each species to serve Him in many ways, allowing them to receive benedictions, but He also personally incarnates in each species.

There are many examples of entities in bodies other than the human form who have received special mercy from the Lord, some of whom are surely worth mentioning. "Ahalya is an example in the body of a stone; the twin Yamalarjunas and the

seven *tala's* in the bodies of trees; King Nrga in the body of a lizard; Bharata Maharaja in a deer's body; Surabhi in a cow's body; Gajendra in an elephant's body; Jamavanta in a bear's body; and Angada and Sugriva in the bodies of monkeys" (*Jaiva-Dharma* xviii). *Perhaps the completion of my existence in material bodies in the material world will soon end, and I will be fortunate to return to the spiritual world to serve eternally as a stone in Vrndavana. I must ask myself, "Am I qualified and ready for this service?"*

While residing in human bodies, I have engaged in devotional service in many different ways. I have been involved in making devotees and helping to maintain their devotional lives. I found unique means to bring people closer to the Vaisnava teachings. I cultivated them personally and tried to create communities that would provide a healthy environment for devotees to cultivate their Krishna consciousness. *Perhaps the completion of my existence in material bodies in the material world will soon end, and I will be fortunate to return to the spiritual world to serve eternally as a stone in Vrndavana. I must ask myself, "Am I qualified and ready for this service?"*

While residing in human bodies, I have been responsible for the building of several temples and the establishment of several schools. In these facilities, people were able to come for worship and education. In the temples, the devotees and non-devotees could have *darsana* of the Deities, hear transcendental discourses, attend festivals, visit or live there as a way to offer services, and have lots of good association. In the schools, devotee and non-devotee children could have opportunities while simultaneously learning academics incorporated with spiritual studies. *Perhaps the completion of my existence in material bodies in the material world will soon end, and I will be fortunate to return to the spiritual world to serve eternally as a stone in Vrndavana. I must ask myself, "Am I qualified and ready for this service?"*

While residing in human bodies, I have been instrumental in establishing several farm communities. In these communities, we tried to emphasize simple living and high thinking. We explored self-sufficiency and tried to create an atmosphere that emphasized unity with diversity. We focused on how to properly address and balance spiritual and material needs. We also tried to prioritize the facilitation of women and children, and encouraged everyone to make loving Vaisnava relationships the number one priority. *Perhaps the completion of my existence in material bodies in the material world will soon end, and I will be fortunate to return to the spiritual world to serve eternally as a stone in Vrndavana. I must ask myself, "Am I qualified and ready for this service?"*

While residing in human bodies, I have established free clinics and outposts for distributing *prasadam* (spiritual foodstuff). These facilities, which offered some of the most basic medical assistance and free food, had much more than just a humanitarian purpose. Such services are most important since we must maintain and care for the body; however, these facilities and programs addressed the whole person—body, mind, and soul. *Perhaps the completion of my existence in the material bodies in the material world will soon end, and I will be fortunate to return to the spiritual world to serve eternally as a stone in Vrndavana. I must ask myself, "Am I qualified and ready for this service?"*

While residing in human bodies, I have been able to preach massively on the television and radio, and have also had contacts with many world leaders. All around the world, I have preached through national television, radio, and newspaper, addressing leadership, relationships, nation building, and social degradation. I have offered ways to re-spiritualize our lives, and solve material problems with spiritual solutions. I have also given workshops and seminars all around the world to devotee and non-devotee communities on these topics and many more. *Perhaps the completion of my existence in the material bodies in the material world will soon end, and I will be fortunate to return to the spiritual world to serve eternally as a stone in Vrndavana. I must ask myself, "Am I qualified and ready for this service?"*

While residing in human bodies, I have distributed many of my spiritual master's books and have written and distributed thousands of my own books in many different languages. Devotees and non-devotees all around the world have been exposed to my style of writing and preaching. In these books, I have tried, in my own little way, to present ancient Vedic knowledge in a lively way to address contemporary issues and concerns. *Perhaps the completion of my existence in the material bodies in the material world will soon end, and I will be fortunate to return to the spiritual world to serve eternally as a stone in Vrndavana. I must ask myself, "Am I qualified and ready for this service?"*

While residing in human bodies, I have nurtured many disciples in connection with all of these other various activities. All of these achievements and endeavors are noble, but secondary. Now the real accomplishment depends on whether or not I have been a proper disciple. If so, I will be qualified and ready to serve in the spiritual world eternally, even as a divine slave. However, I will be just as enthused to serve as a resident of Vaikuntha, or even as a servant in any of the other *rasas* in Vrndavana.

I am that lowly beggar who will depart from these material bodies in the near future and who needs special mercy to become qualified, ready, and satisfied to serve eternally as a stone in Vrndavana.

Meditation 10

Die Before Dying

Just as there is life, there is death. Someone or something takes birth, grows, stays for some time, deteriorates, and then dies. Another name for birth is death. You cannot have one without the other, meaning that when someone is born, someone will soon die (as most species do not live very long); and when someone dies, someone is soon born. Everyone and everything in its normal state wants to live as long as possible—eternally. Eternality, however, is not associated with matter, but is a spiritual affair. Death to matter and to our material bodies is inevitable, but if we master the science of dying before dying, we will connect with

that which is eternal—our soul and its home in the spiritual world. *After all, death is to remove everything false and secondary.*

My mother often used to say, "Give me my flowers while I can still see them." As I child, I thought of it as strange, but as an adult, I saw it as a sign of wisdom. My mother understood the body to be transient and she celebrated life—the "now"—realizing one must show their love and affection for life at every moment. Our life or the lives of others will be taken away in the near future. If we live with proper preparation and detachment, we will master the science of dying before dying to connect with the soul and its home—the spiritual world. *After all, death is to remove everything false and secondary.*

When we die before dying, we put first things first. The activities that nourish our souls and help us detach from the illusion and confusion of material culture are our priorities. Since we know that life is meant to prepare for a glorious death, we can live each day as if it is our last. There is no time to waste on irrelevant, superfluous activities. Even when we must give time to somewhat superficial things, it must be done in a way that enhances the primary, significant involvements. If we live with proper preparation and detachment, we will master the science of dying before dying to connect with the soul and its home—the spiritual world. *After all, death is to remove everything false and secondary.*

There are so many offenses that can be made in devotional services. These offenses are our greatest enemy. Devotional service is extremely potent, but offenses can stagnate our spiritual growth and can even destroy the devotional creeper. Offenses are activities that redirect our consciousness back to previous sinful life or which serve as barriers to our unfoldment. Offenses are like a town courier who delivers an urgent message designed to distract us from our important activities. When we stop making offenses, we will live with proper preparation and detachment. We will master the science of dying before dying to connect with the soul and its home—the spiritual world. *After all, death is to remove everything false and secondary.*

People have cheated, disappointed, lied to, manipulated, and even abused us. When we reflect on each experience, it is as if we relive it again. Such experiences have shaped us in various ways. Many of these abusers and cheaters have traumatized us. In some cases, they have scarred us for life. The normal position is for the hurt or abused to seek revenge and severely punish the offender. It is easy to do, but will not fully resolve the problem. What is important is to address such problems with forgiveness. If we live with proper preparation and detachment, we will master the science of dying before dying to connect with the soul and its home—the spiritual world. *After all, death is to remove everything false and secondary.*

Most people have special people they would like to meet, places they would like to visit, and experiences they would like to have. When we associate with important people, it makes us more important, at least in the eyes of others. When we can travel to many exciting places, life seems to be more adventurous. Most important, when we can have many exciting experiences, life seems more meaningful. We are all pleasure seekers and are always eager to experience pleasure, but the true spiritualist does not get overwhelmed by these concerns, for he understands the temporary and even illusory nature of the world. If we live with proper preparation and detachment, we will master the science of dying before dying to connect with the soul and its home—the spiritual world. *After all, death is to remove everything false and secondary.*

Sometimes we are so busy doing things for those we love that we don't have time to be with them, show them, or tell them how much we love them. Sometimes others are so busy doing things for us that they also have no time to be with us, show us, or tell us how much they love us. However, if we truly understand how this life is a preparation for death, we will always make time to give and receive love.

When someone dies, much of the sadness comes from a lack of sufficient closure in the relationships. There is something we wanted to tell them or do with them, and there is something they wanted to tell us or do with us. Each of us has a tendency to procrastinate on the important opportunities and moments. Especially when a person lives solely for eating, sleeping, mating, and defending, or when the person is captured by a very strong false ego, there is a tendency to miss opportunities to be fully present. The person misses the chance to say or do what will best honor other people's highest needs and blocks the chance for others to honor his or her needs.

Quality association is most important. Where there is quality association, we are always learning something or teaching something. Such association is based on being with those who also are determined to end the cycle of birth, disease, old age, and death. With quality association, we understand that just as there is life, there is death. We act with the knowledge that life is for self-realization, and that death, which is inevitable for matter and the material body, is not associated with the soul. We must die to live! That comes as we accept the inevitability of destruction and elimination of all matter. We can then honor the deaths that have happened and those that are manifesting, knowing that they can prepare the way for eternal life.

The true spiritualist profoundly appreciates my mother's statement, "Give me my flowers while I can see them." Once the body is gone, the soul departs for its new encounter; therefore, it is important to say and do whatever is best for everyone now! Where we have made offenses, we must stop and ask for forgiveness now! While we have people to meet, places to visit, and experiences to have, we must put first things first, understanding the differences between what is temporary and what is eternal now! We must allow every day of our lives to represent healthy closure now! We are most natural when we live for love because all of our associations will be quality associations in which we share our compassion, determination, and realizations, and receive the same from others.

This is the technology of how to celebrate life now and live with proper preparation and detachment, so that we will master the science of dying before dying to connect with the soul and its home—the spiritual world. After all, death is to remove everything false and secondary.

I am that lowly beggar who is desperately trying to die before dying.

Meditation 11

Life Is Simply So Many Breaths

What we call life is really the activities performed by different species as they struggle to avoid their inevitable death. They try to cheat all-devouring death by focusing on eating, sleeping, mating, and defending. It is true that all of these areas are important to maintain for the survival of each species. However, they still do not prevent death from attacking and defeating the members of each species. When someone has few or no obstructions in their eating, sleeping, mating, and defending, it is considered by societal standards that they are having a good life.

As we measure time, we think of how much

longer an entity has in its present body. We reflect on events and activities associated with an entity or entire species. Some species are born, reproduce, and die within twenty-four hours, while other species live for hundreds of years. However, in either case, it is all relative to the nature of the living entity. Life is simply so many breaths. When we take our last breath in this body, the soul departs and petitions for its next existence. The whole of creation simply endures during the breath of Maha-Visnu and is withdrawn when He inhales. *In the spiritual world, there is no deterioration of the body, no death, and no time. Everything has always existed and will always exist. Yes, events and activities are variegated, ever-fresh, full of joy, and eternal.*

The material world is called *kuntha*, a place of misery and anxiety, while the spiritual world is conversely called Vaikuntha, a place of no suffering or anxiety. *Bhaya* or fear pervades all atmospheres in the material universes. This fear is associated with the constant uncertainty about the future, which leads us to try to speed up, slow down, or stop various events from happening. For some, *kala* or time is their best friend because, in time, something wonderful or pleasant will happen. For others, time is their worst enemy, for in the future they will experience some great misfortune. However, for all entities that do not become God conscious, time will prove to be an ultimate enemy in disguise. For those who do not pursue self-realization, they will be chastised and thrown into other material bodies to once again experience birth, death, old age, and disease. Those who become self-realized can return to the spiritual world. *In the kingdom of God, there is no deterioration of the body, no death, and no time. Everything has always existed and will always exist. Yes, events and activities are variegated, ever-fresh, full of joy, and eternal.*

For some unfortunate souls who in the future must experience some specific chastisement, penalty, or difficulty, reflecting on the future brings even greater anxiety and fear. An example is the inmate on death row who has been sentenced to death in one month, or the hostage who receives the news that he or she will be assassinated in twenty-four hours. Even the worker who finds out that, in one week, he must start working with a team of colleagues who will give him hell, will experience tremendous anxiety. Others who anticipate a great boon, reward, or auspicious accomplishment are very excited as they contemplate the future. For example, the prisoner who learns that he or she will be paroled in one month, the hostage who finds out that he can return to his family in twenty-four hours, and the worker who is informed that she will be promoted to the position of a CEO in one week will all feel much happiness. Just imagine how much excitement and happiness the residents of the spiritual world constantly feel, knowing that every future experience will be more rewarding and fulfilling than previous encounters. The more rewarding the future events will be, the greater the anticipation, excitement, and joy. *In the spiritual world, there is no deterioration of the body, no death, and no time. Everything has always existed and will always exist. Yes, events and activities are variegated, ever-fresh, full of joy, and eternal.*

In the material world, as time is ticking away, some people are very excited about a temporary boon, reward, or achievement, while others are in great anxiety about a future chastisement, punishment, or penalty. All will ultimately experience *kala* as most cruel if the real purpose of life is not realized. The ultimate reward will be another material body in one of the material universes that are mainly designed to facilitate the living entities and species in their endeavor to run away from their eternal home—the kingdom of God.

Prahlada Maharaja emphasized that we must not waste this life and its valuable time in just pursuing mundane goals and achievements. Even as a child, we must pursue a more meaningful life. Khatvanga Maharaja became fully God conscious in just moments. We do not have to procrastinate or involve ourselves in superfluous activities. For the materialist who will encounter temporary as well as ultimate punishments, temporary and ultimate anxiety will be their rewards. *But the rewards will be different for the devotees of the Lord who contemplate a future in which they can return to the spiritual world—a place in which there is no deterioration of the body, no death, and no time, where everything has always existed and will always exist. Yes, events and activities are variegated, ever-fresh, full of joy, and eternal.*

All species and entities should use this life for what it is really meant rather than just for eating, sleeping, mating, and defending. Rather than wasting so many breaths and encountering varieties of temporary happiness and distress, we should use life as a divine opportunity to become deathless in a timeless existence where we can eternally participate and breathe in the nectar of *krsna-katha*.

I am that lowly beggar who will soon give up his last material breath to humbly breathe in the nectar of Krishna's divine aroma.

Meditation 12

Let Us Pray to Have Our Bodies Hijacked by the Lord

We regularly hear reports of kidnappings and hijackings. The fear, stress, uncertainty, and anxiety from the encounter engender reflections on our mortality. Whether the victim dies or survives, the trauma from the experience seriously impacts their life. Sometimes the body is kidnapped or hijacked internally by intruding agents, or sometimes it becomes possessed by another entity. This can happen due to a demonic possession in which a negative being imposes its desires on the host. However, a very auspicious "possession" occurs when a divine entity blesses a *jiva* and imposes his or her divine will and blessings on the individual.

Let us pray to have our bodies and consciousness fully taken over by divine influences for this is the greatest boon and blessing.

Sanatana Gosvami once had such a serious illness that his body was oozing moisture from his itchy sores. The disease was trying to hijack his entire body. When Lord Caitanya embraced Sanatana Gosvami, the moisture from the sores got on Lord Caitanya's body, which disturbed Sanatana Gosvami to such an extent that he was even contemplating suicide. When Lord Caitanya discovered Sanatana Gosvami's plan, He chastised him, explaining that he had no right to take his life because his body did not belong to him. Rather, the body is the property of the Lord Himself. This is a reminder for us: Our bodies can become temporarily hijacked or possessed by disease, but ultimately our bodies should be used in the service of the Lord. We should use it only for purposes which please its true owner. *Let us pray to have our bodies and consciousness fully taken over by divine influences for this is a great boon and blessing.*

So many people these days offer their bodies to alcohol and drugs. The intoxicants enter their bodies and infiltrate like an occupying army, gradually destroying not only the physical body, but also having a devastating effect on the consciousness. If a person is not careful, at some point he or she becomes enslaved by addiction. Then his or her entire life will fall under the control of alcohol and drugs. At this point, the person becomes a slave to the intoxicant. Under such influence, the *jiva* will hurt and embarrass those to whom they are closest, and will constantly dishonor themselves. Let us plan our lives in such a way that we will never become prisoners, kidnapped, hijacked, or possessed by intoxications. *Let us pray to have our bodies and consciousness fully taken over by divine influences for this is a great boon and blessing.*

Cancer is a vicious disease that is hijacking and kidnapping millions of bodies. The cancer is alive and very aggressive. It gets stronger and multiplies in a person's body until bringing on a painful death. Cancer seems to particularly manifest due to malnutrition, dehydration, and stress. These enemies first hijack, kidnap, and possess the body, later inviting all kinds of unwanted guests. Melanoma has occupied my own body, but this cancer demon will lose, for my body has been offered to the Lord. Therefore, the Lord will eventually fully claim the body by allowing the cancer to be chased out, or will take me, the soul, out of this sabotaged and diseased shell. Either conclusion is ultimately glorious because the real owner will reclaim His property. Thinking of this gives me great solace. *Let us pray to have our bodies and consciousness fully taken over by divine influences for this is a great boon and blessing.*

Once Nakula Brahmacari's body became divinely possessed by the presence of Lord Caitanya, and thus acquired supernatural powers. One dear associate of Lord Caitanya, Sivananda Sena, who was not at first convinced, challenged Nakula, saying, "If his body is actually divinely possessed, let him tell me what special *mantra* I am chanting?" When Nakula Brahmacari informed him of the *mantra*, he became totally convinced. Lord Caitanya appears in three ways—*saksat, avesa,* and *avirbhava.* The *saksat* is when He appears Himself, *avesa* is when He possesses the form (as in the case of Nakula), and *avirbhava* is when He appears to a devotee although He is not personally present. *Let us also pray to have our bodies and consciousness fully taken over by divine influences for this is a great boon and blessing.*

Sometimes a person's body becomes temporarily hijacked and possessed by what is called shadow ecstasy. This is when he or she is fortunate enough to be in the association of a pure devotee of the Lord. By having this magnanimous, pure association, the potency of that pure soul can sometimes spill over and its wonderful, contagious influences temporarily penetrate the consciousness of the most fortunate *jiva* who is receiving that association. This experience is not permanent, but it gives the *jiva* a glimpse of what can be his or her own divine experience. *Let us also pray to have our bodies and consciousness fully taken over by divine influences for this is a great boon and blessing.*

When Krishna plays His flute, the residents of Vrndavana become totally overwhelmed. The animate entities become paralyzed with ecstasy and *prema*, and the inanimate entities become totally mobile by ecstasy and *prema*. These residents know nothing but Krishna, and He is fully sold out to them. Their love has fully captured the Lord, and His love is their full nourishment. They have hijacked, kidnapped, and possessed each other eternally. This complete divine possession is *divya-mada*, divine madness.

I am that lowly beggar who is praying to soon become totally hijacked, kidnapped, and possessed by Krishna's divine flute for this is the greatest boon and blessing.

Meditation 13

We Will All Very Soon Have a Special Appointment with Death

In late October of 1977, Srila Prabhupada said, "Do things very carefully; I am already dead. But still, I am giving you instructions as far as I can." Through this statement, he was reminding us that he would soon be leaving, but he was also sending a reminder that we are all around the corner from death, and must therefore do the necessary while we can.

Lord Brahma lives for 311 trillion and 40 billion earth years. One day of time according to the demigods is equal to six months of our time. Although Lord Brahma and the demigods live for a long time

in comparison to our situation, it is all relative. They also live up to one hundred of their years, but in every species, death is inevitable. Yudhisthira Maharaja explained that the most wonderful phenomena is how people see others around them dying, but still think that they themselves will never die. People are absorbed in the mundane, living as if they will forever remain in these present bodies. No one is allowed to cancel or postpone their appointment with death when the scheduled time arrives. Neither can someone else sit in for us; we have to personally present ourselves. *We all very soon have a special appointment with death.*

At a funeral home, the bodies of the deceased lie in caskets. Some seem to have a smile on their faces while others seem to have a tormented expression. Some *jivas* leave the body very peacefully with a glimpse of the beauty they will encounter. The helpers who come for them are most divine, pleasant, and refreshing. Others are horrified as the Yamadutas, the superintendents of death in charge of the sinful, come to snatch them out of their bodies. As they perceive their fate, they are petrified. Even though the morticians at the funeral parlor try to make each person's body appealing, it is obvious to all the mourners that the person has been called away to their special appointment. *We all very soon will have a special appointment with death.*

A short visit to the graveyard is even more revealing. One will encounter different types of tombstones and monuments. The grass is manicured, and flowers are lovingly placed over many of the graves. Inscribed in each stone are the date of birth and the date of death. Again we are reminded that just as sure as one is born at a particular time, one will also depart at a designated day and time. Although some of the deceased were wealthy, beautiful, famous, etc., there is little to distinguish one body from another because they are all placed six feet under the ground with dirt piled on top. Some tried to ignore, deny, and yes, even conquer over death, but when the designated time arrived, each person was singled out from millions of other prospective clients. *We all very soon have a special appointment with death.*

Some of the bodies in funeral homes and graveyards died very young and others remained in their bodies for over one hundred years. Some lived in solitude and others had thousands to participate in their funeral ceremony. However, the present differences are less than the similarities because, in each case, everyone who knew them has left them to be alone and has walked away from them, never to associate with that physical body again. As grandfather Bhisma explained on his deathbed, everyone will walk away from us at death and everything will separate from us—only *dharma* or *adharma*, the results of our virtuous or non virtuous acts, will follow us. The deceased in the funeral parlors or in the graves are proof that, in the end, all associates always walk away from us in sadness, fear, and sometimes anger. *We all very soon have a special appointment with death.*

The bodies are disposed of in different ways according to the culture. Some are buried, others are cremated, thrown into the river, or left alone on the mountain or sacred ground to be eaten by vultures and wild animals. Although the final rites vary, the ultimate results are the same: the body will be eaten by worms, insects, fish, or birds, thus returning to the natural elements. *We all very soon have a special appointment with death.*

Some of the deceased died in accidents, some succumbed to disease, some were murdered, some committed suicide and other deaths happened at birth. Whichever way death chooses to call, each person is selected out of billions to leave on a precise day and time under particular circumstances. And in every case, not one person could hide, deny, or postpone their appointment. When death called each client, very few were eager to honor the call. Most had many things to do, to work on, to complete, to finalize, etc. Very few were ready to accept full closure. Most felt that their existence in the body was very short and incomplete.

Of course they are all right. Whether one dies at birth or lives for over a hundred years; whether one had lived in solitude or been very social; whether one had been famous or infamous; whether one had been a material success or failure; rich or poor; sick or healthy; a theist or an atheist, the similarities are that after a short time in the body, we must depart. Even if we consider demigods' time or the lifespan of Lord Brahma in connection with the eternal time associated with the soul, the time we are in these bodies is very short. *No one will have to wait a long time before death specifically calls for them, for we all very soon have a special appointment with death.*

Death has looked in my direction and has pointed at me; her mouth is open. Soon I will see if she is calling my name. I am that lowly beggar who will be called forth now or very soon by death. I pray and beg that when the decision is finally made, I will accept and receive it with excitement and purity. *Let us all get ourselves ready and help others get fully ready for their special appointment with death.*

Meditation 14

The Things We Leave Behind

In the *Srimad-Bhagavatam*, an ancient Vedic scripture, there is a section that describes the character and qualities of Prthu Maharaja. It discusses his very auspicious birth and equates his qualities to other great kings and personalities who preceded him. His death is also simultaneously prophesized. This reminds us of the inevitability of death. When one meets death, one must leave behind many possessions, associates, and other attachments. *However, those who understand the inevitability of death and the eternality of the soul, and who have fully surrendered to the Lord's arrangements will not be disturbed about what is left behind.*

Parents make numerous sacrifices for their children—most would sacrifice their own lives. Nevertheless, when the children start school, go to college, move out, marry, and so on, the parents will have to accept separation. Normally they see their children as their property and as an extension of themselves. People obviously want to stay in control of their properties, but when death comes to the parent or the child, they must honor the full separation. *However, those who understand the inevitability of death and the eternality of the soul, and who have fully surrendered to the Lord's arrangements will not be disturbed about what is left behind.*

It is natural for each living entity to seek out a special partner. Many feel that one day they will in fact meet their soul mate. We are made for love and we are all starving for love. However, what we normally consider love is lust—the fulfillment of our egocentric, selfish desires. Many people spend their entire lives looking for and even waiting for that special person to descend into their lives. Most keep thinking he or she has finally arrived just to later become more and more disappointed. A few who do seem to find that special lover become even more upset, sad, and disappointed when he or she ultimately dies. The more wonderful the connection, the more painful the permanent separation. *However, those who understand the inevitability of death and the eternality of the soul, and who have fully surrendered to the Lord's arrangements will not be disturbed about what is left behind.*

Most people spend the majority of their quality hours working at their jobs. Instead of *having* a job, people often think that they *are* their jobs. Perhaps they have studied very hard to become competent in their profession, made many huge sacrifices, passed many tests, and accomplished outstanding achievements. However, at some point in the near future when death comes, the job and all things associated with it will be left behind. *However, those who understand the inevitability of death and the eternality of the soul, and who have fully surrendered to the Lord's arrangements will not be disturbed about what is left behind.*

In today's society, it is so important to have a functional, secure residence. The mortgage payments, repairs, taxes, and other costs involved in the maintenance of a home can be extremely demanding. The larger and more opulent the house, the more care and attention it demands from the owners. Not only does a home require interior decoration, the owners must clean it or have it cleaned regularly. The apartment, house, or mansion is like a very greedy, demanding living entity who is never satisfied and always waiting for service. Although owners give special care to their residence and spend decades acquiring things to decorate the house, when death comes, they will have to permanently separate from their residence. *However, those who understand the inevitability of death and the eternality of the soul, and who have fully surrendered to the Lord's arrangements will not be disturbed about what is left behind.*

There are others who give more attention to decorating their bodies. They have closets full of clothes and drawers full of jewelry, cosmetics, and other items. Such people keep up with the latest styles, love to shop, and love to make others envious of what they wear. Some are not only obsessed with what they put on their bodies, but what they do to their bodies as well. They may go on many diets, exercising religiously, while others may visit plastic surgeons regularly for modifications and adjustments. Regardless, no matter how much they decorate and modify the body, the end result is massive deterioration and death. *However, those who understand the inevitability of death and the eternality of the soul, and who have fully surrendered to the Lord's arrangements will not be disturbed about what is left behind.*

The hardest attachment to leave behind is wealth and close friends; they are somewhat similar. We identify ourselves according to our possessions, especially our finances. We feel secure or insecure due to our financial status, as our money and financial assets are connected with the confidential aspect of our lives. Just as we share so many confidential things with our closest friends and they with us, and just as when one is facing various difficulties, there will still be some solace when one remembers his or her stocks, bonds, gold, diamonds, or real estate that can be accessed when needed. Close friends serve the same purpose: they are on reserve, waiting and available to assist in any way they can. It is hard for most people to appreciate existence without both of these confidants, but some time in the near future when death calls, we will all have to leave behind these highly valued supports, securities, and intimate friendships. *However, those who understand the inevitability of death and the eternality of the soul, and who have fully surrendered to the Lord's arrangements will not be disturbed about what is left behind.*

I am that lowly beggar who will also die in the near future, who will leave possessions, associates, attachments, and relationships behind. You have prepared me to not be disturbed by what I leave behind, for I will take your prayers and love with me.

Meditation 15

Why Be Afraid of Death?

Today my soul spoke to my temporary self and said, "Hey, what is this? How can one with so much knowledge be afraid of death? Death is one of Krishna's most loyal subjects. Death is equal to all and does not forget or pass anyone up. Death is often very patient; she may wait 100 or more years before appearing, but she can also take the *jiva* away in seconds. Death removes everything that is false; death reveals to us our true friends; death exposes our true priorities; death brings forth wisdom; death educates us on our fears and weaknesses; but, most importantly, death reminds us that these material bodies and material universes are not

our homes. *Since death is calling you, don't fear or hide, but present yourself and see what she has to offer. After all, she is a just, faithful, and loyal servant of Krishna.*"

My soul said, "Maybe you are afraid of suffering the pain that is often associated with death. We may not mind a particular person coming to visit our home, but we do not like the company they keep. Another example is Lord Siva who is a first class devotee, but he is often in the association of all kinds of abominable characters. Dear friend, it is often the suffering and pain that engenders our greatest realizations. What often appears as suffering or poison is like nectar at the end:

> *yat tad agre visam iva*
> *pariname 'mrtopamam*
> *tat sukham sattvikam proktam*
> *atma-buddhi-prasada-jam*

That which in the beginning may be just like poison but at the end is just like nectar and which awakens one to self-realization is said to be happiness in the mode of goodness.

Bhagavad-gita 18.37

"Since death is calling you, don't fear or hide, but present yourself and see what she has to offer. After all, she is a just, faithful, and loyal servant of Krishna."

My soul inquired, "Are you afraid because of your previous failures? When death came for you at a time when you were not qualified to return to the kingdom of God, you were chastised by Yamaraja, the superintendent of death. Yamaraja and his attendants keep very good records; they were fully aware of your shortcomings in previous lives. After all, in *Bhagavad-gita*, Krishna explains how people who worship in different modes enter into different destinations at the time of death.

> *yanti deva-vrata devan*
> *pitrn yanti pitr-vratah*
> *bhutani yanti bhutejya*
> *yanti mad-yajino 'pi mam*

Those who worship the demigods will take birth among the demigods; those who worship the ancestors go to the ancestors; those who worship ghosts and spirits will take birth among such beings; and those who worship Me will live with Me.

Bhagavad-gita 9.25

"Since death is calling you, don't fear or hide, but present yourself and see what she has to offer. After all, she is a just, faithful, and loyal servant of Krishna."

My soul continued, "Are you afraid because you are thinking that you will miss your present relatives, friends, students, disciples, and projects? Or are you feeling that they will all miss you and they need your physical presence to continue? Let me remind you that you have died thousands of times and so have they. Your spiritual master used you to assist him in his mission, and Krishna often educated and guided you in the heart. So what you have accomplished was due to them. Just as they used you, they can use others, and just as you were given service on this planet, your next services have already been arranged. Remember, Krishna says in *Bhagavad-gita* 2.27:

*jatasya hi dhruvo mrtyur
dhruvam janma mrtasya ca
tasmad apariharye 'rthe
na tvam socitum arhasi*

One who has taken his birth is sure to die, and after death one is sure to take birth again. Therefore, in the unavoidable discharge of your duty, you should not lament.

"Since death is calling you, don't fear or hide, but present yourself and see what she has to offer. After all, she is a just, faithful, and loyal servant of Krishna."

My soul continued to explain, "I see your greatest fear of death is your fear of loosing yourself, as you are my temporary and illusory associate. You must have great fear of our departing since we have done everything together. However, you have frequently been under the illusion that you are the doer and the controller. Each time you visited the superintendent of death, he tried to remind you that in your next existence, you must stop trying to lord over all that you survey and that you must give up the pursuits for adoration, prestige, and other subtle attachments. Several times you came back to another material body and again became entangled as a controller rather than fully depending on *guru* and Krishna. Sometimes you became so involved in trying to spread Krishna consciousness that you minimized simply being Krishna conscious.

"You should reflect on the fact that it is not death that is to be feared but material existence. Those who think they are alive but who are really dead are the real ones to fear because they create pain, suffering, failure, and confusion all around them. They create wars, crimes, abuse, and the exploitation of others. They maintain a culture of eating, sleeping, mating, and defending. They are attacked repeatedly by various miseries known as *adhyatmika* (miseries arising from one's own body and mind), *adidaivika* (miseries or natural disturbances caused by the demigods), and *adhibhautika* (miseries caused by other living beings).

"So beloved, be afraid of living a so-called life that is void of real spirituality for such a life is no life, but is worse than death. Do not worry about suffering or pain, for if they do accompany death, they will not stay around very long. Tolerate them and absorb whatever realizations they bring you. Your previous failures are now your foundation, which have presently given you a strong footing; they are assets in disguise. As far as you missing others and them missing you, once again remember how Krishna says in *Bhagavad-gita* 2.12:

> *na tv evaham jatu nasam*
> *na tvam name janadhipah*
> *na caiva na bhavisyamah*
> *sarve vayam atah param*

> Never was there a time when I did not exist, nor you, nor all these kings; nor in the future shall any of us cease to be.

"As far as you having incoherence about your projects and things to complete, remember that if these projects are a genuine offering to *guru* and Krishna, they can choose to accept the offerings at any point they want. It is not up to you when and how they choose to respond. Lastly, as far as your biggest fear of loosing your identity—your self, remember that Krishna says in *Bhagavad-gita* 2.26:

> *atha cainam nitya-jatam*
> *nityam va manyase mrtam*
> *tathapi tvam maha-baho*
> *nainam socitum arhasi*

If, however, you think that the soul [or the symptoms of life] is always born and dies forever, you still have no reason to lament, O mighty-armed.

"Therefore, beloved friend, it is this duality that you must transcend. For instance, we are now somewhat separate with two identities due to your doubts, attachments, and fears, but now that death is calling, we must join together as one. You will soon connect fully with me and we will return as one to our home and services in the spiritual world. Many of our associates are assisting you with this transition; you are stubborn, but nevertheless blessed. Now give up all fear of death. *Since death is calling you, don't fear or hide, but present yourself and see what she has to offer. After all, she is a just, faithful, and loyal servant of Krishna's.*"

I am that lowly beggar who has a short time to renounce all duality so as to greet death with celebration.

Meditation 16

The Nine-fold Process
of Full Surrender

My soul, feeling all my anxieties, felt this was a good time to intervene. My soul said, "Why are you in so much anxiety about whether you live or die. If you live, what will you continue to do? Devotional service, of course! If you die, what will you do? Devotional service, of course! So, *jiva va mara va*: 'Either you live or you die, as you like.' Whether you live or die, it is okay because there is so much service waiting for you. Whether you stay in this same physical body or change bodies, your spiritual master has already arranged your assignments. *Your anxiety should be how to please guru and Krishna, and how to get freed from your separation from them.*

"You are in great anxiety about your medical care and treatments. Sometimes you are disturbed by the side effects of the drugs and, at other times, you are overwhelmed by the amount of medication you must digest in tablets, liquids, and injections. And yet at other times you are in anxiety, wondering how long you must continue with these protocols? Why not be in more anxiety about *sravanam*, hearing the transcendental message of *bhakti-rasa. Your anxiety should be how to please guru and Krishna, and how to get freed from your separation from them.*"

My soul reported, "You worry each day if the cancer has spread to other organs of the body, and how seriously affected are those organs. Are you forgetting that the whole material body is diseased? Sometimes the diseased state of the body is very obvious, but sometimes not. When it is more obvious, it reminds us of its temporary nature, helping us to become less absorbed in it. You should be in anxiety about *kirtanam*, chanting the glories of the Lord. As one calls on the Lord's name with sufficient purity, reciprocation is immediate. *Your anxiety should be how to please guru and Krishna, and how to get freed from your separation from them.*"

My soul continued, "You are in so much anxiety about your extremely austere diet, and sometimes you do not even have an appetite. Sometimes you reflect on all of the wonderful things you used to eat, but as your body ages, it is natural for you to be more alert about what you eat and drink. This is why you should be more in anxiety about *smaranam*, remembering the pastimes of the Lord and His servants. By remembering them, a devotee gets their association. *Your anxiety should be how to please guru and Krishna, and how to get freed from your separation from them.*"

My soul now exclaimed in an almost hilarious spirit, "It is obvious you are in anxiety due to having lost so much weight and to not being able to sleep peacefully at night. These experiences are surely an indication of the limitations and harassments of the physical body. During the night when your foot, which is infiltrated by cancer cells, gives you more trouble, you must use these experiences to focus on *pada-sevanam*, serving the lotus feet of the Lord. *So don't forget that your anxiety should be how to please guru and Krishna, and how to get freed from your separation from them.*"

My soul kept on talking, knowing that I have a short time to understand all that is necessary. He said, "You are very anxious about not being able to travel and preach. You have traveled around the world several times giving lectures, seminars, and workshops. You should not worry about this so much. More important than what we speak is how we live and what consciousness we maintain. You should be more concerned with *arcanam*, worshiping the Deity of the Lord. Even when you cannot be physically available to others, you can use this as a time to take more shelter of service to the Deity. The Deities know our most personal desires and needs, and are most merciful to Their sincere servants. *Therefore, your anxiety should be about how to please guru and Krishna, and how to get freed from your separation from them.*"

My soul very mercifully tried to help me more by explaining, "I know that one of your worst fears is to die a slow, painful death. Already there are times when you want to cry out to *guru* and Krishna that you cannot bear this anguish another day. However, you should be more anxious about taking shelter of *vandanam* or prayer. Prayers are such an intimate connection with *guru* and Krishna. Through prayer, you can present your case before the Lord and beg Him to allow His will to manifest. If it is His will for a slow, painful transition, let it be so, for our worshipable Lord only arranges what is best for the *jiva* who is fixed deeply in profound, internal prayer. So once again I remind you: *Your anxiety should be how to please guru and Krishna, and how to get freed from your separation from them.*"

My soul stared at me while saying, "You are very afraid of being forgotten by the *sadhus*, but this is a foolish concern. First of all, we should never be eager for fame, adoration, and distinction. Secondly, we should always remind ourselves that all services are really an offering to *guru* and Krishna, and they are both fully aware and appreciative of unconditional service. They are the best friends and well-wishers of everyone. It is better for you to be more anxious about *dasyam* and *sakhyam*, being a humble servant and desiring friendly, appreciative service to and association with the Lord. *After all, your anxiety should be how to please guru and Krishna, and how to get freed from your separation from them.*"

My soul slowed down his speech as if to make sure I heard and internalized each of his words. He said, "My beloved Bhakti Tirtha Swami, who is no different than myself, once all fear, attachments, and false ego are destroyed, we will be fully united as one soul eternally serving the Divine Couple. Please give up your anxieties about whether you live or die, or how long you must continue with difficult treatments and their side effects. You must give up all fears about the cancer spreading. Do not give any more energy to worrying about diet, weight loss, or loss of sleep because you are ultimately headed towards trading in this harassing limited body for a new spiritual one. Lastly, do not worry about dying with excruciating pain and being forgotten. Your illness is a sign of *guru* and Krishna's special and personal mercy being extended to you. Your outcome has already been arranged; your prayers were heard and accepted even before they left your mind. All you have to do now is focus more on *atma-nivedanam*, full surrender. You have spoken about, written about, and constantly heard about the power of full surrender. Now the day and time has come where *atma-nivedanam* is knocking on your front door. Just as I have been telling you: *Your anxiety should be how to please guru and Krishna, and how to get freed from your separation from them.*

"Very soon, by the mercy of your spiritual master, you will be lovingly forced to embrace full surrender. So be joyful and radiant, because only moments away, your life, or better to say your death, will be successful.

"Yes, my darling, you are that lowly beggar whose prayers have been heard and accepted."

Meditation 17

Being on Death Row

Having terminal cancer is a death sentence. It compares to a prisoner who has been convicted and sentenced to death. The person on death row experiences similar symptoms to those suffering from a life-threatening disease—shock, anger, grief, self-pity, and depression. Each day is an intense struggle in the dealings with his or her fate. The inmate knows that the warden has arranged an exact day and time for his demise. *However, the self-realized soul is not in the least bewildered by his impending death; he sees the appointment with death as a victory and graduation ceremony.*

The prisoner on death row knows that many

have been sentenced to death before him, and in the future there will be others. He wonders what each person did that warranted execution, and what their last few days and hours were like. He thinks of how easy it is for a person to make a mistake that can destroy his own life or the lives of others. It can take a very long time to mature, grow, and build up a project, career, or life. Nevertheless, in a few minutes all of these accomplishments can be destroyed once a person makes such a mistake. Serious consequences will follow, even death. *However, the self-realized soul is not in the least bewildered by his impending death; he sees the appointment with death as a victory and graduation ceremony.*

Just as in the case of the critically ill, sympathizers may visit to express their grief, support, and condolences. Of course they all mean well, but often their bewilderment and sadness put the patient in an even more sad and helpless state. Although the prisoner and critically ill are happy to receive guests who are thoughtful, loving, and caring towards them, at the same time they are not so eager for those close to them to witness their current precarious position. When such companions do visit with them, all are reminded of the prisoner's or the patient's impending death. *However, the self-realized soul is not in the least bewildered by his impending death; he sees the appointment with death as a victory and graduation ceremony.*

Each day both the prisoner on death row and the critically ill patient are praying for a miracle. The person with a critical illness is hoping that by some miracle the disease goes into remission or that some special medicine or doctor will save his or her life. The prisoner is praying that his appeal will be accepted; that some new evidence may come; or that through some miracle he will be pardoned. They try to keep this little flame of hope burning until their actual, inevitable death. *However, the self-realized soul is not in the least bit bewildered by his impending death; he sees the appointment with death as a victory and graduation ceremony.*

The prisoner on death row and the critically ill person often wonder how they got into their present devastating condition. They both start looking back at their lives wondering what he or she could have done differently. They have many flashbacks of wonderful encounters and experiences, but, at the same time, they are aware of their many foolish behaviors. They realize now that if they were able to live their lives over again, they would do many things differently. In several cases, their priorities would change now that they face their death, but it is too late. *However, the self-realized soul is not in the least bit bewildered by his impending death; he sees the appointment with death as a victory and graduation ceremony.*

The prisoner is offered a choice for his last meal, but just as in the case of the critically ill, food no longer seems to nourish the body, for one may either have no appetite or may be beyond having a need to eat anything. Both people realize the futility of trying to nourish the body, as it is on a fast path to annihilation. However, before being sentenced to death or before coming down with the critical illness, most of the person's waking hours were focused on stimulating the physical body. Impending death confronts one with how temporary and fragile the body is. Death is a destructive but powerful teacher. *However, the self-realized soul is not in the least bit bewildered by his impending death; he sees the appointment with death as a victory and graduation ceremony.*

The prisoner on death row and the critically ill wonder what their last thoughts will be as they get called out of their bodies by death. In most cases they are not aware that the consciousness at death will determine their next body:

yam yam vapi smaran bhavam
tyajaty ante kalevaram
tam tam evaiti kaunteya
sada tad-bhava-bhavitah

Whatever state of being one remembers when he quits his body, O son of Kunti, that state he will attain without fail.

Bhagavad-gita 8.6

The way in which a person has lived and the aggregate of his or her thoughts at the time of death will form a result, which will help direct the soul to its next destination. *However, the self-realized soul is not in the least bit bewildered by his impending death; he sees the appointment with death as a victory and graduation ceremony.*

The condemned prisoner and the critically ill wonder who will be there with them when they take their last breaths. Life is an accumulation of breaths. People normally waste so much energy as they engage in frivolous conversations. Instead of engaging in *krsna-katha* (talks about the Lord), they pursue *gramya-katha* (mundane discussions). As we are mindful of our thoughts, our speech will become more palatable and constructive. Proper thoughts produce proper speech, which produces proper actions, which produce proper habits, which will produce a proper culture. Presently, most people are addicted to their culture of material sense gratification. Therefore, when something inauspicious happens to their bodies, they become totally frustrated. *However, the self-realized soul is not in the least bit bewildered by his impending death; he sees the appointment with death as a victory and graduation ceremony.*

When that final appointed time arrives and the soul departs from the body, what was once alive simply becomes a corpse. For the condemned prisoner as well as the critically ill person, the body must be disposed of according to tradition, religion, culture, situation, and condition. As everyone walks away from the body, enemies, strangers, friends, and family will all leave, never to see it again. Death brings closure to one's existence in the previous body and changes the relationships that previously existed. Only the spiritual connections will permanently remain with us. Therefore, so much of what we normally hold on to and see as most significant is not only temporary but will walk away from us. Whether one is on death row, subjected to critical illness, or dies of old age, everyone was sentenced to death the day they were born. Everyone must prepare him or herself for the appointed day. *However, the self-realized soul is not in the least bit bewildered by his impending death; he sees the appointment with death as a victory and graduation ceremony.*

I am that lowly beggar who is on death row waiting for either a miracle of divine intervention or a victorious departure.

Meditation 18

We Must Die for Ourselves

One way we define our existence is by what we offer to our community, how we are valued and perceived by our community, and how participation in our community enhances our God consciousness. Normally we begin by getting nurtured by our families; we attend different schools; join clubs and organizations; associate with like-minded people; or attend social, cultural, political, and religious functions. In other words, much of who we are, what we do, and who we are becoming is based on our associations within the community. The most amazing thing is that although we are social beings who are evaluated by others, ultimately we must do the most important things in our lives ourselves. Others cannot do them for us, and sometimes we must do them alone. *Death especially clarifies this for everyone.*

When the living entity takes birth, each soul must make the journey of connecting with parents and later enter into the world through the birth canal. There are many helpers that visit us in the birth process, some material and some spiritual. Higher beings help determine the exact conditions that the soul is to experience, and the material bodies, eggs, and sperm that are needed. Once all of these arrangements are in place, the living entity continues his or her journey of maturation. *Death especially clarifies this for everyone.*

The body, being a machine, needs proper care. When it is sick, it needs proper food, proper environment, proper herbs, and proper medicines to assist with restoration. The body also needs proper sleep; without proper sleep the body falls apart in many ways. Just as no one else can take the medicines that we must take to restore our bodies, no one else can take rest for us when our bodies experience fatigue. Their sleeping will not restore our bodies. The same goes for eating. No one can eat for us; it is our bodies that need the nourishment. *Death especially clarifies this for everyone.*

Sometimes for school or for a job, we may have to take examinations. Usually these tests are given to see how much we know, or how competent we have become. These tests reveal our strengths along with our weaknesses. The test is to bring clarity to us as well as to others—our exact status. We also take physical examinations to evaluate the condition of our health. No one else's exam scores or health analysis can substitute for ours; we must have our own evaluations. *Death especially clarifies this for everyone.*

Even as basic and mundane a thing as going to the toilet cannot be relegated to someone else. No matter how busy, absorbed, intelligent, or powerful one may be, when a serious call for elimination descends, no one can permanently avoid the call, and no one else can eliminate for him or her. Someone else's elimination will not alleviate our own need. *Death especially clarifies this for everyone.*

More basic is our breathing. We take thousands of breaths in one day's time. Most of us exhale and inhale mechanically without any encumbrance or cognizance. However, if we loose our ability to breathe for just a few minutes, our life is in danger. Someone or some machine may be used to help us restore our natural breathing, but ultimately, in order to continue with our healthy lives, we must be able to breathe ourselves. Even if those who love us or those trying to save us are breathing nicely, they cannot transfer their normal breathing to us. Inevitably, they must do their own breathing and we must do ours. *Death especially clarifies this for everyone.*

The path of *bhakti* is to give up sinful life, to avoid unhealthy sense gratification. Each *sadhaka*, aspiring devotee, who associates in the community of devotees must make their own vows for fellowship and worship, must maintain their commitments, and must perform their own devotional services. Here again, each person must undergo their own test to reestablish their pure relationship with the divine couple, Mother-Father God. Each aspirant must individually transform their lower taste to the higher taste of transcendental activity.

Friends, family members, and even mentors can pray for, coach, and guide us, but still we must individually involve ourselves in the process of surrender. Everything we read, hear, see, remember, feel, talk about, associate with, etc. should help us work more expediently on our individual spiritual acceleration. If our own quality is not improving, we will cheat others, and cheat ourselves even more. *Death especially clarifies this for everyone.*

Just as each individual has his or her own unique fingerprints, we are all individually unique in many ways. Sometimes when a person undergoes a routine operation, the doctor may not anticipate any complications, but the patient develops many problems. Other times, by all rational scientific evaluations the person has no chance of survival; however, they may experience spontaneous remission and go on to lead a very healthy life. We see in such cases that we all have an appointed time to die. Until that time manifests, nothing can force it on us, and when the time does come, no one can stop it. Death especially reminds us of how we are unique. Death reminds us that we each have our own appointments and specific relationships with God. Our deaths are just as controlled by higher authorities as our births.

Yes, it is true that we are social beings who survive in community. It is through community that we define ourselves and reawaken our dormant consciousness. However, we must eat and sleep for ourselves, pass our own examinations, breathe ourselves, do our own elimination, perform our own *sadhana*, and most important we must do our own dying. *Death especially clarifies this for everyone.*

I am that lowly beggar who is prepared to do his own dying. I thank the community of saints for assisting me in preparing for this solo journey.

Meditation 19

Death Can Be the Perfect Escape

Death is a Vaisnavas' Victory Celebration! Therefore, upon the death of a Vaisnava, festival arrangements are made. Friends and family come together to reflect on the many good qualities of the deceased, discussing the wonderful ways he or she impacted their lives. The individual's departure is glorious because a serious devotee goes back to Krishna, joins his *guru*, or is commissioned to perform higher services with even better association in his or her next life. Even if such a devotee does not fully graduate from having to enter into material bodies again, still his or her next life will be more auspicious. A healthy life is the goal of the devotee saint, for in death the devotee aligns or reconnects with eternal life and service. *Death offers the soul a chance to make the final escape from all illusions and material incarcerations.*

The living entity, due to misuse of free will and enviousness of God, temporarily tries to become a master of the relative, transitory, illusory world of duality. Such an entity is given the chance to feel disconnected from transcendence in a place where he can try to become the Supreme, making ridiculous efforts to lord over all that he surveys. In these attempts to enjoy and find happiness, the living entity simply contemplates the objects of the senses, and forms sequences of acts leading to negativity. "While contemplating the objects of the senses, a person develops attachment for them, and from such attachment lust develops, and from lust anger arises" (*Bhagavad-gita* 2.62). The living entity, after experiencing extreme failures, setbacks, and frustrations, one day meets a bona fide spiritual mentor. He is informed that by expertly following these instructions, he gets the full mercy of his *guru*:

> *tad viddhi pranipatena*
> *pariprasnena sevaya*
> *upadeksyanti te jnanam*
> *jnaninas tattva-darsinah*

> Just try to learn the truth by approaching a spiritual master. Inquire from him submissively and render service unto him. The self-realized souls can impart knowledge unto you because they have seen the truth.
> *Bhagavad-gita* 4.34

The *guru* helps escort him out of his bodily imprisonment. *Death offers the soul a chance to make the final escape from all illusions and material incarcerations.*

When the living entity undergoes the process of birth, it has a traumatic experience in the womb. The embryo is bitten by worms and inconvenienced by whatever the mother does. The poor being is cramped into a little sack, not knowing his future while subjected to intense suffering. A mature adult could never endure such suffering. But the worst is yet to come, for when the little being is forced out of the womb covered by blood and placenta, he is introduced once again to a life of physical and emotional sufferings. It is only upon death that the *jiva's* incarceration can be fully terminated. *Death offers the soul a chance to make the final escape from all illusions and material incarcerations.*

While in the physical body, living entities struggle individually and collectively at their most basic level. Their energy is focused on *annamaya,* simply evaluating the environment and looking for what is edible. Once the hunger is somewhat satisfied, then the individual becomes a little more involved, now focusing on *pranamaya* or arranging for protection and security. When this drive is somewhat fulfilled, the entity now pursues *manomaya* or intellectual pursuits and inquiries. If the *jiva* moves through these stages properly, he will advance to the stage of pursuing *vijnanamaya* and *anandamaya,* self-realization and transcendence.

All of these stages involve tremendous work and subject the *jiva* to complex anxieties and sufferings. If one does not come to the stage of *anandamaya,* one is likely to once again enter into material bodies in the material world. Most global citizens rarely progress past *annamaya* or *pranamaya*, and most current governments and civilizations rarely mature past the first or second levels of survival and existence. *However, death offers the soul a chance to make the final escape from all illusions and material incarcerations.*

Life is a constant series of setbacks, tests, and challenges; as soon as we successfully pass one test or recuperate from a particular setback, another test, challenge, or calamity appears. Some people give up by committing suicide, becoming mentally depressed or just accepting defeat and mediocrity. Others, who think they are still independent creative agents, are often docile, controlled, and imprisoned by fads and propaganda. Those who are imprisoned by these societal norms think that they are genuinely enjoying, but are actually even more imprisoned than those who are aware of their struggles, suffering, and pain. Being too comfortable in the material body is a disqualification for transcendence. *Difficulties can aid us in moving through the stages of development more seriously, and death offers the soul a chance to make the final escape from all illusions and material incarcerations.*

When a person dies, the destination of the soul varies. Some *jivas* wake up and find themselves in their original *svarupa* looking very blissful and youthful, fully prepared to serve the divine couple in intimacy. When others leave their bodies, they find themselves having the same form as the Lord. And yet other *jivas*, due to the nature of their worship, go to reside in various abodes that correspond with their worship or lack of worship. *Death offers the soul a chance to make the final escape from all illusions and material incarcerations.*

The living entity is sometimes like a carefree spontaneous lovely wild animal that has been captured and forced into a cage. The cage is extremely confining, imposing all kinds of unnatural limitations on the *jiva*. Most *jivas* begin to know the boundaries and limitations as normal because, after all, everyone around them is confined as well. When prisoners remain in a cage for a long time, they begin to forget that there is any other existence than what they are presently experiencing. Therefore, one accepts and adjusts to such a monotonous, restricted, and artificial life.

From time to time, the pure devotees and even the Lord Himself come to rescue them, but more often than not, they are so entangled, covered by such illusions and absorbed in immediate gratifications and problems that they miss out on the mercy that is extended to them. The great souls unlock the door of *samsara*, repeated birth and death. They try to point to the path of escape but unfortunately most of those who are incarcerated do not understand the wonderful opportunity being offered to them. Some rare souls, when coming in contact with the Lord and His special representatives, become fully attentive, joyful, and appreciative. These rare souls perceive the Lord and His envoys as the path for escape. After being sufficiently coached, they run full speed out of the prison cage never to look back or return. If they do return, it is not as a prisoner, but as a warden or more likely as a merciful guide who is eager to help escort the imprisoned *jivas* out of their horrific suffering and confinement.

These guides fully understand the nature and intensity of each prisoner's sufferings and are extremely empathetic. But even more important is that each guide is fully aware of the glorious life outside of the prison that is awaiting every *jiva* who has a successful escape. Anyone who accepts the full guidance of the Lord and His most special agents will have their most special escape. *We want, beloved, to constantly remind ourselves and others that death offers the soul a chance to make the final escape from all illusions and material incarcerations.*

I am that lowly beggar who has been blessed by the Lord and His envoys. They have opened my prison cell, come inside to coach me, and now have invited me to come and join them. Will I follow immediately or will I postpone the invitation? And if I postpone it, will I remain able to perceive the path?

Meditation 20

Cancer: An Offering of Tough Love

Cancer is alive. Like any living entity, survival is of foremost importance. It is a natural instinct for people to organize their lives around trying to maintain their existence. My cancer is definitely life-threatening to my physical body. The medications and treatments I am taking are designed to kill the cancer cells so it is natural for them to fight just as hard to survive. All life ultimately comes from Krishna, God, so all life has its purpose and can offer a learning experience. *Today I want to send my love to the cancer, for after all everything is for our benefit. Thank you so much cancer cells for offering me tough love.*

The cancer has helped me in connecting on a much deeper level with my biological family. We are all so different but were brought up very similarly by my mother who was most thoughtful, kind, and considerate. When she passed from ovarian cancer, we bonded very strongly as a family in prayer and support. When my brothers and sisters heard of my seemingly fatal disease, they all flew in to spend some quality time with me. We discussed so many important issues, and prayed, laughed, and cried together. In all cases, we were fully there for each other. *Today I want to send my love to the cancer, for after all everything is for our benefit. Thank you so much cancer cells for offering me tough love.*

By the mercy of Srila Prabhupada, my spiritual mentor, I have been brought in contact with a beautiful and diverse spiritual family of godbrothers and godsisters. These wonderful servants have made most amazing sacrifices year after year. All over the world, they have spread the teachings of *sanatana-dharma*, sacrificing wealth, health, family, education, and prestige. Several of them are now aging and even passing away. During this sickness, I have been in touch with spiritual godfamily from all over the world. We have connected on deeper levels as servants in Srila Prabhupada's mission more than ever before. Of course, we are also wondering who amongst us may be next to leave his or her body. This has helped us all look closer at our own health and most significantly to reexamine how much we need and depend on each other. *Today I want to send my love to the cancer, for after all everything is for our benefit. Thank you so much cancer cells for offering me tough love.*

By the mercy of *guru* and Krishna, I have been

given so many loving disciples. They are praying for me daily, organizing special *pujas, yajnas,* and other ceremonies. Most have raised their own standards and made greater commitments. They are coming together as a spiritual family more than ever before, and trying to hold on to my instructions. They are reaching out to make each other more accountable. They are taking shelter of more spiritual uncles, aunties, and others for *siksa.* They are sending me more love than ever before. They are reading my books, listening to my tapes, and listening to Srila Prabhupada's tapes more seriously than they have during their entire spiritual journey. When I was healthy, they were attentive, but nowhere near as much as they are now. *Today I want to send my love to the cancer, for after all God does not make mistakes and He arranges everything for our benefit. Thank you so much cancer cells for offering me tough love.*

This seemingly fatal disease has caused me to look closer at my own attachments, gross and subtle. It has very clearly been put in front of me what needs to be transcended before returning back home. The cancer has allowed me to be much more appreciative of what I have previously experienced and accomplished. It has increased my appreciation of the wonderful years of excellent health that I had most of my life. It has allowed me to look closer at what is really important in contrast to what is superficial or secondary. It has helped me to be more mindful of each moment and each encounter. It has clearly shown me how much I am not in control of my life nor was I ever. This has surely made me more dependent on *guru's* and Krishna's mercy. The uncertainty and desperation the cancer has produced is giving me a wonderful chance to detach myself from my bodily identifications and to search out more connections with my eternal permanent identity. *Today I want to send my love to the cancer, for after all God does not make mistakes and He arranges everything for our benefit. Thank you so much cancer cells for offering me tough love.*

The cancer has helped me better understand the sufferings others have to endure. I had prayed desperately to become a more empowered agent of change, so as to understand their suffering. I wanted the ability to help others deal with, grow from, or move through their pain. Now it is no longer an academic experience, but it is experimental. The seemingly fatal disease has helped me to develop a deeper level of wisdom and compassion far beyond what I normally possess. This has also allowed me to reflect and write with greater sensitivity with hopes that I will connect on a deeper level with the hearts of my readers. *Today I want to send my love to the cancer, for after all God does not make mistakes and He arranges everything for our benefit. Thank you so much cancer cells for offering me tough love.*

My dear cancer cells, you are a messenger. A messenger who brings honest, accurate, bad news should not be faulted, even though the truthful news is unpalatable. A messenger has the duty to deliver the precise message. You have done a very good job as a courier. The message has reached its destination. I have received it in full, and I am acting upon it with intense haste and gravity. This wake up call has helped me to look closer at Lord Caitanya's last prayer:

aslisya va pada-ratam pinastu mam
adarsanan marma-hatam karotu va
yatha tatha va vidadhatu lampato
mat-prana-nathas tu sa eva naparah

I know no one except Krishna as my Lord, and He will always remain as such, even if He handles me roughly by His embrace or makes me broken-hearted by not being present before me. He is completely free to do anything and everything, for He is always my worshipable Lord, unconditionally.

It is easy to be appreciative and grateful when everything happens in our lives according to our desires. However, the real test of our faith and love comes when we have challenges and setbacks that are confusing. It can bewilder us even more when the Supreme Himself seems to allow or arrange such sufferings, or when He may seem to handle us roughly or not be present before us. However, all of what the Lord does is best for our coming back to Him. So this chronic disease has given me a better understanding of unconditional, unmotivated service. It has helped me move faster towards embracing unconditional love towards *guru* and Krishna and more genuine service and appreciation for all *sadhus*.

My beloved cancer, you must also die; you either die with me or before me, but neither of us can remain forever in these hellish bodies. So, there is no longer any need for us to be enemies, for our ultimate outcome with material nature is the same—it destroys us. This is a time of giving thanks, for I am so appreciative of the many wonderful things you have brought to me. Now you must die, and I must also eventually die; in both of our cases our time is very limited. Therefore, once again I want to send you love and appreciation for all the wonderful things you have added to my life. *Especially today, I send my love to you, the cancer, for after all God does not make mistakes and He arranges everything for our benefit.*

I, the lowly beggar, again thank you cancer cells for offering me tough love.

Meditation 21

Live Until Dying

I do not know how long I have to live in this present body, due to terminal illness. Surely I am near death, or perhaps I will have died by the time you, my beloved, read these prayers. Even if I, your loved ones, or you survive a terminal illness, death will still make an appointment with each of us in the near future. So, yes, we are all born to die. If we can die even before dying by understanding the temporary nature of the material body and the eternality of the soul by turning ignorance into knowledge, lust into love, selfishness into selflessness, enviousness into appreciation, and hatred into compassion, we will die to live. By bringing death to ignorance, lust, selfishness, enviousness, and hatred, we will gain our rightful claim to inherit and live in the kingdom of God. *Rarely do we know the exact time of our death, but even if we do, still we must live until dying.*

In the past I have had a few very good astrologers offer me readings after learning the particulars of my birth. They have all agreed that I am more an entity of the future and that my life would begin to accelerate with greater and greater achievements after 55 years of age. They expressed how I will have international influence over communities, world leaders, etc., which would grow until I step back from all of this in my 80's to enter into *nirjana-bhajana* (a state of consciousness where one no longer relates to the temporary material body and world). Well, I am now 55 years old and, yes, I already have contact with many world leaders and some basic influence with several international communities. However, as I write this last meditation, it seems that my visit to this material world and my stay in this limited material body is over. Perhaps due to a higher influence, these readings are now wrong. *Rarely do we know the exact time of our death, but even if we do, still we must live until dying.*

Fifteen million children under the age of five die every year worldwide, two hundred children die of cancer in a day in the United States, three teenagers commit suicide every day, 115 people die each day in car accidents in the United States, fifty-two deaths occur each day in Australia as a result of smoking, and this short list barely covers the thousands of people in the world who die every day from all types of other causes. Whatever the cause or the means by which a person dies, the ultimate result is the same: everyone must give up his or her body after a short time of occupancy. Many people worry so intensely about events of the past. These events haunt and attack the individual just like a ghost who keeps appearing. Others live in the past because their present is too disturbing or challenging while others live in the future, romantically wishing for a utopia because their past and present are too disturbing. Both of these groups cheat themselves and others, for they miss the chance to experience the present in fullness. *Just like someone who has phobias about dying in a certain way or at a certain time, we should constantly remind ourselves that rarely do we know the exact time of our death. Even if we do, still we must live until dying.*

People are very different when they believe they will soon die. Some will increase their bodily identification and attachments by trying to experience as much sensual gratification as they can before giving up the body. Some become paralyzed by depression, self-pity, fear, and anger. Others see it as a time for the soul to connect more with its true eternal identity, fully accepting the inevitable while living with gratitude in the present. Such rare souls understand the science of dying to live, dying before dying. *Rarely do we know the exact time of our death, but even if we do, still we must live until dying.*

Even if a person leaves the body very early, this should not present a problem if we die before dying because we would have lived in the present to our very best, learning from the past while joyfully anticipating the future. Some of the greatest personalities left the body at an early age. Jesus left at 33 years of age, Sankaracarya at 32, Lord Caitanya at

43, Martin Luther King Jr. at 39. Sometimes the body dies seemingly untimely; however, the higher authorities know how long each of us is to remain incarcerated in these material bodies. When our time is up, they come to assist us out of the body. Some souls are blessed to leave early, as they do not have to stay long in their present imprisonment. The most fortunate ones return back to the spiritual world because they have obtained liberation. If we live a long or short life, we must nevertheless be ready to die before dying and to die to live. *Rarely do we know the exact time of our death, but even if we do, still we must live until dying.*

In the Vedic scripture *Srimad-Bhagavatam*, Maharaja Pariksit knew he only had one week to live, and Maharaja Khatvanga only moments. Grandfather Bhisma in the *Mahabharata*, lying on his deathbed of arrows, also had only moments to live. Jesus at the last supper knew he only had days, what to speak of the founder of ISKCON, His Divine Grace A.C. Bhaktivedanta Swami Prabhupada and other great *acaryas*. How did they all respond? Did they get angry with the Supreme Lord, wonder why, lose faith, or go out and engage in as much sensual gratification as possible? No, on the contrary, they all intensified their meditation on the Lord, accepting the Lord's plan with great faith and dedication. Ultimately they knew that they were fortunate to be singled out to engage in special services for their worshipful Lord, and they were ready to be called for more accelerated services in this or other realms. *As I have continually expressed, rarely do we know the exact time of our death, but even if we do, still we must live until dying.* We must live with honor and die with even greater honor for death is the greatest opportunity for ultimate success.

I am that lowly beggar who will live until dying, who is praying to die to live eternally in the kingdom of God.

Beloved, thank you for living with me through these meditations. Now you die before dying, die to live, and most importantly, live devotionally, fully in the present until your own death. If you are most fortunate, when you give up this body you shall also return to the spiritual world, the kingdom of God, to live eternally in full knowledge and bliss.

By the mercy of the Lord, my divine spiritual master and their sweet loving messengers, I am that lowly beggar who has died before dying.

So what is service proper? Hegel's philosophy is: Die to live, dissolve your ego as it is at present. Dissolve it mercilessly, die. Die means to dissolve mercilessly. Throw yourself into the fire and you will come out with a bright self. Learn to die as you are: That mentally concocted body, that concocted energy. To take the name of the Lord and die. Forget yourself as you are at present and you will find your proper self there that does not die. Death is ordained for our existence, so give to death that part of you that is ordained to die, and the eternal part of you will remain. Not only physical death, but real death, the wholesale death, is necessary.

- Srila Bhaktisiddhanta Sarasvati Thakur, quoted in the *Journal of Sri Gaudiya Vedanta Samiti, No.10, Summer 2002*

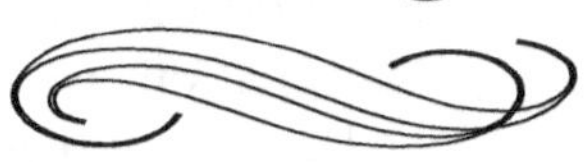

In my own life I've recently discovered the value of watching my mind and observing where it seeks shelter during life's tests. Do I become angry and blame others? Do I eat, shop, turn on the radio, or just become busy? Embarrassingly—and sadly—I've noted my shelter is often neither Srila Prabhupada nor Krishna nor Vrndavana nor Nitai nor Gaura. Nor, often, is it Krishna's holy names called out loudly and sincerely in my true need. Philosophy may easily roll from the tongue, but its ultimate test is whether or not it carries us to a true shelter—the lotus feet of Krishna and His dear ones. In this way, life prepares us for death, the ultimate test.

Indeed, Srila Prabhupada has quoted the Bengali proverb *bhajana kara sadhana kara mrtyu janle haya*: Whatever *sadhana* and *bhajana* you are performing will be tested at the time of death. In Vrndavana in 1975 he said, "It will be test. Just like a parrot is chanting, 'Hare Krishna, Hare Krishna,' but when some cat comes in, 'Kaw, kaw, kaw.' No. Parrot life will not help you. You must be really chanting without any offense. Then it is a possibility at the time of death... Death will be there."

And in London in 1973 when he spoke that same proverb, he again evoked the image of a parrot: "You may be very great devotee. That's all right. But it will be tested at the time of your death, how you remember Krishna. That will be the test examination. At the time of death, if we forget, if we become parrot-like… Just like parrot, he chants also, 'Hare Krishna, Hare Krishna, Hare Krishna.' But when the cat catches the neck, 'Kaw! Kaw! Kaw!'' No more Krishna. No more Krishna."

Unlike a parrot, a devotee who has firmly fixed Krishna as his shelter, is known as a surrendered soul. That fixedness in surrender to Krishna, according to Srila Bhaktivinoda Thakura in his *Harinama Cintamani*, is the *svarupa-laksana* of a *sadhu*, his primary characteristic.

His Holiness Bhakti Tirtha Swami, a surrendered devotee and *sadhu*, has kindly allowed us glimpses of his consciousness in this book, *Die Before Dying*. Maharaja is also a preacher, through and through and until the end. He, as a preacher, as a servant to his followers, and as a friend, has offered an account, a journal in the form of a series of meditations, that will aid our own passage at that most difficult time—our own death. And he has done this with honesty, deep insight, and open-hearted power. Clearly Maharaja is also preaching to himself, and by doing so, his own conviction and depth of prayerful dependence are strengthened.

What we have read in this book, the fourth written in his *Beggar* series, is a set of meditations on his approaching death. Each makes powerful and touching reading. Bhakti Tirtha Maharaja wrote them in the late months of 2004 after he had been diagnosed with terminal cancer and had more or less exhausted all avenues of treatment. Slight hope remains, however, but that too rests in Krishna's hands. He has even quite openly admitted in his preface that he may not live to see this book published.

Bhakti Tirtha Maharaja's strength, faith, humility, and nurturing affection for others flow thickly through *Die Before Dying* like sweet honey. As I read his meditations, which in his own style and mood examine his own consciousness, I note that his doing so has caused me to freshly examine my own. Do I pursue spiritual life selfishly? Have I escaped the dangers inherent in my preaching successes? With what do I ultimately identify? Can I possibly positively view forced renunciation of past, present, and future? Can relationships have life in the face of one's impending death? What do I wish as my life's ultimate accomplishment?

Bhakti Tirtha Maharaja's approach to his own death is not unlike an expert jeweler's examination of a diamond. Under his careful eye, through his scrutiny, sparkling facets of Krishna consciousness are revealed, many of which would have remained unseen by me. In his acknowledging that "death is, after all, a faithful loyal servant of Krishna," he teaches how to die. And in his doing so, Bhakti Tirtha Swami teaches us how to live.

Thank you Maharaja for awarding me, a reader, transparent access to you, Bhakti Tirtha Maharaja the person, a brave and devoted soul as you face that which no one wishes to face—your own death. I will miss you Maharaja, and I pray to remain in remembrance of you by keeping this book with me as a companion.

— His Grace Bhurijana dasa Adhikari

Appendix A

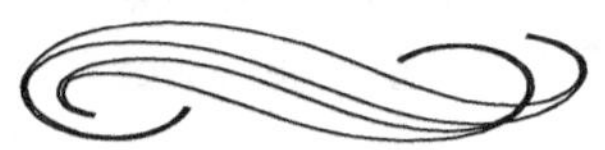

Take the Name of the Lord and Die

I always seem to be worrying about my creditors. Fully absorbed in obtaining money, once I get it, I find myself anxiously watching how fast it leaves me. It really seems as though I'm working for other people. The more I get, the more I want. The more I make, the more I spend. Where is there peace in this world? Where is the happiness I was promised? *Hearing me screaming, my spiritual master said, "My dear son, scream on, but TAKE THE NAME OF THE LORD AND DIE!"*

Just as I think I am pulling ahead of my mortgage payments, something happens and I get further behind. Watching the bills pile up, I realize I am nothing more than a slave to this building. Sometimes I do not see how I can continue to have a house to live in. I work like a dog outside its walls and like a menial servant inside. What an ungrateful master! *Hearing me scream so pathetically, my spiritual master said, "My dear son, scream on, but TAKE THE NAME OF THE LORD AND DIE!"*

What kind of life is this? I waste so much time

grooming my body, getting my hair just right. I buy clothes that are very attractive, but very uncomfortable. Every pair of new shoes I put on is like a unique form of torture, as my feet feel they are in a vice. And this is fashion?

I jump into my new car, which I can only drive on very special occasions simply because I can't afford the gas. I make all this effort to attend a social gathering at which I find myself completely miserable. Why have I made such a fool of myself to attract the attention of other fools and rascals? *Hearing me scream in frustration, my spiritual master said, "Yes, scream on, but TAKE THE NAME OF THE LORD AND DIE!"*

Sometimes I spend from morning to night trying to do something to improve my health. I do all types of exercises, and have tried all forms of medical treatments for an interesting array of diseases. Not one cure has ever lived up to its promise, except the promise to leave me poorer and more frustrated than when I started. As for my so-called specialists with their perfect knowledge, I find them simply in need of money. So they grow richer at my expense. *Hearing me scream out angrily, my spiritual master said, "You TAKE THE NAME OF THE LORD AND DIE!"*

Sometimes I feel I am being haunted by my past. I have had so many bad habits. I have engaged in all types of sinful activities. I have offended so many saintly souls. I have given the worst treatment to those who loved and cared for me the most. I have broken all religious principles and even tried to deny the existence of God. I see the faces of all those I have offended, hurt, and denied, shouting out at me. All of my bad habits come before me again and again, taunting me as if I never left them.

How long must I be haunted like this? *Hearing me scream in agony, my spiritual master said, "My dear son, scream on, but TAKE THE NAME OF THE LORD AND DIE!"*

Sometimes I think of the future and I become very alarmed. I have suffered so much in the past and I am afraid that more of the same is waiting for me. Since I cannot bear my present miseries, how will I be able to brave what is waiting for me in the future? Past, present, future—for me they are all the same, full of hellish despair. There is nothing to be excited about in this world, as ultimately everything ends in frustration. Life is a role in a bad play, then the curtains close in one's face and the show is over, soon to be forgotten. *Hearing me scream so pitifully, my spiritual master said, "Scream on, but TAKE THE NAME OF THE LORD AND DIE!"*

"My dear son," He continued, "you are realizing the absurdities of this material world. This material world is designed solely for your rectification. When one is no longer satisfied in the prison, such a person becomes eligible for liberation. As long as one is comfortable in these universes of great limitations and duality, there is no hope of escaping. Your realizations and frustrations are all a part of the price one pays to be released. Please do not turn back; please keep up the intensity, as your freedom will be upon you very soon. The holy names of God are not of this world. By chanting these divine sounds vigorously, one can unlock the doors of the material prison and return back home, back to Godhead. Scream on, my dear child, but take to the chanting of the names of God. This will bring death to the old attachments, illusions, sufferings, and fears, and will bring in the real life of eternal happiness and bliss. With serious chanting, my child, you can ride the wind!

"Put the things of this world behind you and now live in truth and love. Take the name of the Lord in full absorption and eternal life is yours. *Don't waste a second. Yes, you must TAKE THE NAME OF THE LORD AND DIE!*"

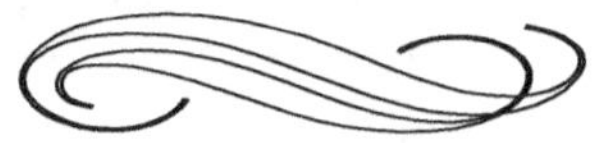

Die to Live

My dear Lord Nityananda, I am not qualified to consider myself a mentor, a saint, or even a serious student. Still I position myself for Your mercy. Pleading for Your guidance, and knowing myself unworthy of Your blessings, I ask for Your empowerment, protection, and even salvation. As You are the most merciful, I will grasp this opportunity and, falling at Your feet, put my full life before You. My humble request is that You make me a pure mentor. Since You never turn anyone away, I know in time You will even accept a lowly puffed-up pretender like me. Since I have nowhere to go, how can I leave Your shelter? Please instruct me so that I will not remain in embarrassment.

The Lord gently spoke mercifully but firmly, "My dear child, it is very simple. If you want to become worthy of My full guidance and blessings, you must *DIE TO LIVE*!

"Someone tries to get My blessings while still attached to family life. Taking shelter and solace with wife, husband, children, and other relatives, he makes them his number one priority. I say to such a poor fool: You must *DIE TO LIVE*!

"Someone is trying to get My guidance and blessings but is attached to beautiful women. Daily he visits the marketplace of the female form, studying the vendor's wares. He shops closely, electing the best items to take home and enjoy to his full satisfaction. I say to such a poor fool: You must *DIE TO LIVE*!

"Someone is trying to get My guidance and blessings but is so proud of his education. Eager to show off his mundane learning, he flaunts his various degrees, not understanding that the only things he has "mastered" are speculation and misinformation. I say to such a poor fool: You must *DIE TO LIVE*!

"Someone is trying to get My full guidance and blessings but is so eager to have many friends and admirers. He judges the success of his life by the approval of his friends, undergoing hardships and making sacrifices to earn the respects of his foolish peers. I say to such a poor fool: You must *DIE TO LIVE*!

"Someone is trying to get My full guidance and blessings but lusts after wealth. Struggling to secure funds, he makes a habit of cheating and stealing. He makes nothing a priority unless he sees some way to profit from it. Thus he has no serious enthusiasm to work. I say to such a poor fool: You must *DIE TO LIVE*!

"Someone is trying to get My full guidance and blessings but his attempts to approach me is overshadowed by a deep hankering for followers. Preoccupied with fame, distinction, and adoration, he craves the title "great devotee." He engages in ridiculous activities solely to win others to his camp. I say to such a poor fool: You must *DIE TO LIVE*!

"Someone is trying to get My full guidance and blessings but is so attached to mundane duty. Being truthful and righteous, he enjoys hearing everyone know that he is a righteous man. He does not realize that one may go on for millions of years in this way and still never become qualified for My blessings. I cannot be fooled nor am I impressed by one's austerities or performance of so-called routine responsibilities. I say to such a poor fool: You must *DIE TO LIVE*!

"Someone is trying to get My full guidance and blessings by being very religious. I have allowed these religions to exist just to awaken the moral, ethical, and pious spirit in man. These are but some prerequisites in becoming a godly person, but are only elementary. Such a person goes from church to church, temple to temple, mosque to mosque, and book to book, thinking that I can be found in an institution or through philosophical speculation. I am known only through My pure devotees. I say to such a poor fool: You must *DIE TO LIVE*!

"My dear child," He went on to say, "even Lord Brahma, the most intelligent personality in your universe, had to die to live. Earlier he had experienced bewilderment. Confused and lonely, he made mistakes in performing his creative duties. Even worse, he became so overwhelmed by the desire for sex that he chased after his own daughter. He had to give up his body before he was able to receive proper mercy from Me. Therefore, my child, you, who are full of sinful desires, far from the intelligence of Brahma, should try to understand the need to give up your illusions, misconceptions, attachments, and false ego along with your subtle body. My guidance and full blessings are available to everyone, but to qualify, *YOU MUST DIE TO*

LIVE in pure unadulterated, unmotivated, loving service to Me, because it is through such death that you will truly live!"

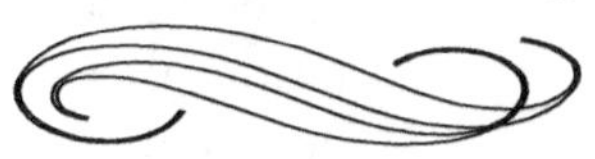

Acarya: A spiritual master who teaches by his own example, and who sets the proper religious example for all human beings.

Adharma: Irreligion.

Adhibhautika: Misery caused by other living beings.

Adidaivika: Misery or natural disturbances caused by the demigods.

Adhyatmika: Miseries arising from one's own body and mind.

Aisvarya: The Lord's majestic, opulent aspect.

Annamaya: Consciousness absorbed only in food.

Arcana: The procedures followed for worshiping the *arca-vigraha*, the Deity in the temple; engaging all the senses in the service of the Lord.

Artha: Economic development.

Atma-nivedanam: The devotional process of surrendering everything to the Lord.

Bhajana: Intimate devotional service; chanting devotional songs in a small group, usually accompanied by musical instruments; solitary chanting.

Bhakta: A devotee of the Lord; one who performs devotional service (*bhakti*).

Bhakti-yoga: Devotional service to the Supreme Lord.

Bhava: The stage of transcendental love experienced after transcendental affection; manifestation of ecstatic symptoms in the body of a devotee.

Bhaya: Fear.

Darsana: The act of seeing or being seen by the Deity in the temple or by a spiritually advanced person.

Dasyam: The devotional process of rendering service to the Lord.

Dharma: Religious principles; one's natural occupation.

Gosthy-anandis: A Vaisnava who is interested in spreading Krishna consciousness.

Gramya-katha: Literally means 'village talk'. Refers to unnecessary and superfluous discussions about worldly matters.

Guru: Spiritual master.

Hladini-sakti: Krishna's pleasure potency.

Jiva: A spirit soul.

Jnana: The path of empirical knowledge, culminating in attainment of impersonal liberation (*sayujya-mukti*).

Kala: Eternal time.

Kama: Lust.

Kirtanam: Glorification of the Supreme Lord; the devotional process of chanting.

Krsna-katha: Discussions or topics spoken by or about Krishna.

Manomaya: Consciousness absorbed in mental activity.

Maya: The external energy of the Supreme Lord, which covers the conditioned soul and does not allow him to understand the Supreme Personality of Godhead.

Mayavadis: Any person who thinks that the name and form of the Supreme Lord are made of *maya*, or material energy; ultimately, *maya-vadis* want to merge into the impersonal Brahman (*sayujya-mukti*), thereby committing spiritual suicide.

Moksa: Liberation from material bondage.

Pada-sevanam: Service to the lotus feet of the Lord; one of the nine principal limbs of devotional service.

Pranamaya: Consciousness absorbed in maintaining one's bodily existence.

Prasadam: Sanctified food; food offered in devotion to Lord Krishna.

Prema: Love; pure and unbreakable love of God; the stage after *bhava*, where the soul has attained both self-realization and God realization.

Puja: Worship, usually in the form of making offerings to the Deity of the Lord.

Rasa: The transcendental "taste" of a particular spiritual relationship with the Supreme Lord.

Sadhaka: One who practices regulated devotional service.

Sadhana: Systematic practices aimed at spiritual perfection, especially Deity worship and chanting the holy name of the Lord.

Sadhu: A saintly person.

Sakhyam: The spiritual mellow of friendship; one of the nine principal limbs of devotional service.

Samsara: The cycle of repeated birth and death in the material world.

Sanatana-dharma: The eternal activity of the soul; the eternal religion of the living being which is to render service to the Supreme Lord.

Siksa: Transcendental instructions received from
the *guru* through the *parampara*.

Smaranam: The devotional process of remembering the Supreme Lord; constant thinking
of Krishna (one of the nine methods of devotional service).

Sravanam: Hearing from an authorized source;
the chief of the nine methods of devotional
service.

Svarupa: The living entity's original eternal relationship of service to the Lord, the real form
of the soul.

Svarupa-laksana: The principal symptom (i.e.
surrender to Lord Krishna) of a *sadhu* regardless of *varna* and *asrama*.

Vairagya: Renunciation; detachment from matter
and engagement of the mind in spirit.

Vandanam: The devotional process of offering
prayers to the Lord.

Vipralambha: Ecstasy in separation.

Virya: Strength.

Vrajavasi: A resident of Vrndavana.

Yajna: Sacrifice.

Yasah: Fame.

About the Author

Bhakti-Tirtha Swami Krishnapada was born John E. Favors in a pious, God-fearing family. As a child evangelist he appeared regularly on television. As a young man he was a leader in Dr. Martin Luther King, Jr.'s civil rights movement. At Princeton University he became president of the student council and also served as chairman of the Third World Coalition. Although his main degree is in psychology, he has received accolades in many other fields, including politics, African studies, and international law.

Bhakti-Tirtha Swami's books are used as reference texts in universities and leadership organizations throughout the world. Many of his books have been printed in English, German, French, Spanish, Portuguese, Macedonian, Croatian, Russian, Hebrew, Slovenian, Balinese and Italian.

His Holiness has served as Assistant Coordinator for penal reform programs in the State of New Jersey, Office of the Public Defender, and as a director of several drug abuse clinics in the United

States. In addition, he has been a special consultant for Educational Testing Services in the U.S.A. and has managed campaigns for politicians. Bhakti-Tirtha Swami gained international recognition as a representative of the Bhaktivedanta Book Trust, particularly for his outstanding work with scholars in the former communist countries of Eastern Europe.

Bhakti-Tirtha Swami directly oversees projects in the United States (particularly Washington D.C., Potomac, Maryland, Detroit, Pennsylvania, West Virginia), West Africa, South Africa, Switzerland, France, Croatia and Bosnia. He also serves as the director of the American Federation of Vaisnava Colleges and Schools.

In the United States, Bhakti-Tirtha Swami is the founder and director of the Institute for Applied Spiritual Technology, director of the International Committee for Urban Spiritual Development and one of the international coordinators of the Seventh Pan African Congress. Reflecting his wide range of interests, he is also a member of the Institute for Noetic Sciences, the Center for Defense Information, the United Nations Association for America, the National Peace Institute Foundation, the World Future Society and the Global Forum of Spiritual and Parliamentary Leaders.

A specialist in international relations and conflict resolution, Bhakti-Tirtha Swami constantly travels around the world and has become a spiritual consultant to many high-ranking members of the United Nations, to various celebrities and to several chiefs, kings and high court justices. In 1990 His Holiness was coronated as a high chief in Warri, Nigeria in recognition of his outstanding work in Africa and the world. In recent years, he has met several times with then-President Nelson Mandela of South Africa to share visions and strategies for world peace.

In addition to encouraging self-sufficiency through the development of schools, clinics, farm projects and cottage industries, Bhakti-Tirtha Swami conducts seminars and workshops on principle-centered leadership, spiritual development, interpersonal relationships, stress and time management and other pertinent topics. He is also widely acknowledged as a viable participant in the resolution of global conflict.